# Hey, History Isn't Boring Anymore!

## A Creative Approach to Teaching the Civil War

by
Kelly Ann Butterbaugh

WHITE MANE KIDS
SHIPPENSBURG, PENNSYLVANIA

Copyright © 2008 by Kelly Ann Butterbaugh

ALL RIGHTS RESERVED—No part of this book may be reproduced in any form without permission in writing from the publisher, except by a reviewer who wishes to quote brief passages in connection with a review.

Photographs are by the author.

The acid-free paper used in this book meets the guidelines for permanence and durability of the Committee on Production Guidelines for Book Longevity of the Council on Library Resources.

    For a complete list of available publications
    please write
    White Mane Kids
    Division of White Mane Publishing Company, Inc.
    P.O. Box 708
    Shippensburg, PA 17257-0708 USA

Library of Congress Cataloging-in-Publication Data

Butterbaugh, Kelly Ann, 1974-
  Hey, history isn't boring anymore! : a creative approach to teaching the Civil War / by Kelly Ann Butterbaugh.
    p. cm.
  Includes bibliographical references and index.
  ISBN-13: 978-1-57249-395-7 (pbk. : alk. paper)
  ISBN-10: 1-57249-395-X (pbk. : alk. paper)
  1. United States—History—Civil War, 1861-1865—Miscellanea—Juvenile literature. I. Title.
  E468.9.B895 2008
  973.7—dc22
                                                                                            2008020363

PRINTED IN THE UNITED STATES OF AMERICA

*To my son Christopher,*
*may you always find life fascinating*

# Contents

| | |
|---|---:|
| Following the Code of the Civil War Soldier | 1 |
| Civil War Personality Quiz | 9 |
| Pieces of the Quilt | 19 |
| Fiction or Fact? | 31 |
| Letters to Home: The Words of a Civil War Soldier | 39 |
| Which Is Which? North versus South | 45 |
| Sherman's March through Georgia | 51 |
| Civil War Trivia | 61 |
| The Battle of Bull Run | 67 |
| Know the Famous Names of the Civil War | 73 |
| The War at Sea | 77 |
| Twenty Questions about the Civil War | 81 |
| Acknowledgments | 87 |
| Notes | 89 |
| Bibliography | 91 |
| Educational Resources | 93 |
| Index | 105 |

# Following the Code of the Civil War Soldier

Whether one called himself Union or Confederate, wore gray or blue, or fought for the North or the South, he was still a Civil War soldier. When the war was young, the soldiers thought it offered a touch of adventure to their lives, but as it dragged on, they soon learned that life as a soldier wasn't so easy. See if you could lead the life of a Civil War soldier.

*Every day you come home from school, have a snack, and start your homework. After that you eat supper, watch TV, and then head to bed. Not too interesting, right? Imagine that one day at school a man comes to speak to your class about volunteering to take part in his program—the adventure of a lifetime. Those who are involved will perform a duty in protecting their country and preserving the rights of its citizens. When the trip is over, you'll return as a hero. While on this trip you won't be able to talk to your family, but the entire thing shouldn't last more than three months. Are you interested?*

This is the scenario that many soldiers of the Civil War imagined when they heard recruiters talk about joining the army. The soldiers would return home as heroes in three months' time. Little did they know this was not the vision they would soon be seeing.

2 Following the Code of the Civil War Soldier

The 23rd Pennsylvania Volunteer Infantry "PA-23rd / Birney's Zouaves," a member of Vincent's brigade, march past the Union soldiers as they salute their victory during a reenactment. The Zouave troop wears a unique uniform that reflects its French influence.

Their time of enlistment was ninety days because it was believed that the war would be over in such a short time period. It lasted for four years, and many soldiers did not return home. Many who did were often severely wounded or maimed. The armies attracted many men who were bored with their simple lives and sought adventure. Away from home they would march endlessly and suffer from the heat of summer and the cold of winter. Homesickness was the greatest illness of the war.

*For years you have been watching the school's baseball team play, and you desperately want to be a part of it. However, everyone on the team needs to be at least fifteen to play, and you're only twelve. Then, one day you see a smaller boy tagging along with the team. Watching him you realize that he isn't a player on the team; he's the bat boy who is in charge of the equipment. He doesn't bat or catch or run the bases, but he does get to be on the field and be part of the team. Do you run to ask the coach if you can sign on as a bat boy, too?*

This is how young boys took part in the battles of the Civil War. Soldiers needed to be at least eighteen years old and five feet five inches tall to enter the army. However, many tall sixteen-year-olds sneaked by wary recruiters' eyes. The lure was so great that it is estimated that 10 to 20 percent of all the soldiers were under eighteen when they joined, earning the Civil War the nickname "the boys' war."[1] Only fourteen at the time, William Cain drilled new recruits in the 25th North Carolina while attending Hillsboro Military Academy.

While many boys lied about their age to pass as soldiers, others did it honestly. They were known as the drummer boys of the Civil War. The job of a musician, drummer, or bugler wasn't to fight; therefore, many recruiters didn't bother with age requirements of these enlistees. Drummer boys as young as ten were known to march with the soldiers. According to the rules, they were not allowed to take part in the combat, although there are many stories of those who did. Either way, they were part of the army.

Drummers were essential to the army. They served as a way for the army to communicate with its members through gun smoke or the cloak of night. There were estimated to be 40,000 musicians in the Union army and 20,000 in the Confederate army, and so many of them were young enough that the job was called "drummer boy" or "bugle boy."[2] The Civil War was the last war to use drummers as part of the army.

*Everyone in your family boasts of their years spent in college. Not only did they attend college, but they all attended the same college. Mother, father, uncle, grandfather, they all attended the same campus with the same name. You have a few years before you graduate, but already you feel as though it is your duty to attend the*

The fife and drum players lead a Confederate reenactment troop back to camp. After a loss in battle, the fife offers to lift the soldiers' spirits as they return to their families and tents.

# Following the Code of the Civil War Soldier

same college. Although you would like to attend a trade school instead, you give in to the fact that you will follow in the family's footsteps. After all, college offers summers off and plenty of fun and activities. (Forget about the hours of studying and hard work that would come first.) Do you make the announcement that you will become the third generation to attend the ivy league school, or do you break the news of your future plans of trade school gently?

By the time the Civil War was into its first year, the soldiers knew that the ninety day enlistment was a thing of the past. Yet, the lure of the war still brought them to enlist. Often they did it because of a feeling that it was their duty to enlist and fight for their country. Like college, the army seemed rewarding. The soldiers would return as heroes, and they would enjoy the excitement of battle. Instead, they realized that a soldier's life included more marching and waiting than battle, and they drilled endlessly. Many young men covered their heads to protect themselves from musket fire as they lay sprawled upon the earth thinking of their quiet lives back home.

*After a successful season your soccer team made it to the state championships three hundred miles away from your hometown. You played as hard as you could, but your team lost the match. It was a hard fight, but in the end the winning team showed great sportsmanship in congratulating you for a job well done. In all the excitement after the game you somehow missed your bus home, and now you are stranded miles away from home. There is no one you can call for a ride, and you are in the midst of strangers. What do you do?*

This is the same question Confederate soldiers asked themselves at the end of the Civil War. After four years of fighting, they were exhausted and starved, not to mention suffering from low morale. The Union soldiers had won the war; the Confederate soldiers had not.

A Confederate soldier bites the cartridge and another takes aim during a reenactment at Twin Grove Park.

Union soldiers were rewarded well for their victory. Each corps was broken into smaller groups that were then shipped home. Each man, and sometimes woman, who had fought for the Union army or navy was paid a final sum of pay and given transportation home. Many were involved in parades in Washington, DC, as well. However, many of these soldiers celebrated quietly. There was a solemn honor at the end of the Civil War while Northern soldiers respected the fighting of their Southern brothers. The North had won the war, but the true victory was that it was over.

Confederate soldiers met the end of the war in a different way. For them the war ended, and they were abandoned where they had last fought. With no food and little money, there was no last pay for these men. They simply turned in their weapons and were left to find their ways home. Some Northerners helped; Generals Ulysses S. Grant and William T. Sherman gave their food stock to the Southern soldiers, and the Northern states offered transportation to some areas. For most of these soldiers,

Union soldiers mock salute after a win.

however, their only path home would be found walking, often for hundreds of miles. Along the way the farmland was as devastated as the soldiers, and no one had food to give to the men. Perhaps the harshest end of it all was that they had to walk through the land that had been destroyed by the war—their homeland, for there were no grand feasts or parades welcoming the Confederate soldiers home.

# Civil War Personality Quiz

Have you ever wondered what it would be like to meet one of the people who took part in the Civil War? History books only allow us to know them for their historical contributions and the events of their lives, but what were they like in person? Their friends and families knew them well, and they had the chance to see these people outside of their fame. Although it's too late to get to know them personally, take this personality test to see if you fit the profiles of a few famous names of the Civil War.

**Compassionate**

*Do you have a soft spot for animals? Is the sight of a lost puppy too much for you to bear? Do you enjoy the simple times spent with family?*

*If so, than you're a compassionate person.* Compassion is having the feeling of concern and love towards another thing or person. A compassionate personality puts others first and tries to understand how it would feel to be them. Innocent or helpless people or things attract a compassionate person's attention, and he would not hesitate to stop to help them.

Robert E. Lee would fit this type of personality, although he may not want to admit it. Known for being a driving leader who led the Confederate army, Lee is lesser known for his compassionate ways. However, he certainly had such a side, even as a general.

When Robert E. Lee's children were young he would pile them in bed with him and read stories. However, while he was reading, the children had to tickle his feet. If they stopped, he would tell them, "No tickling, no story."[1] Does this sound like the determined leader of the Confederate army?

It may not sound like it, but this is the compassionate side of a determined Confederate leader. While traveling, Lee kept his pet hen with him at all times. She would sleep beneath his bed and ride beside him in his wagon as he led his troops across the countryside. When the battle of Gettysburg was over and Lee was leaving, his hen was nowhere to be found. He and several of his men set up a party to search for her, and only once she was found did Lee and his wagon leave the battlefield.[2]

Lee's love for animals surfaces in several lesser known events during the Civil War. Amid enemy fire at Petersburg, Lee was seen dismounting his horse to replace a baby bird who had fallen from his nest.[3] Likewise, during the battle of the Wilderness, one messenger rode to deliver Lee a message. Upon delivery Lee scolded the man for riding his horse too hard and informed him of the proper way to care for the animal. He then produced a buttered biscuit from his saddlebag and gave it to the poor animal.[4] This compassion for animals also transferred to people.

While in battle, General Lee always made his camp from tents. He refused to disturb those who lived in the area by occupying their homes as his base. Instead, he used the tents, which were simple and often rather crude for the leader of an entire army. In the fashion of his simple lifestyle while in battle, Lee played chess on a homemade chess board with simple pieces that did not resemble the chess pieces of today.

General Lee's headquarters still stand in Gettysburg, Pennsylvania, and are available for tours.

**Determined**

*Do you fight to get things accomplished at all costs? Are you persistent in your beliefs despite any complications? Do you stand up for those being abused by others, and do you refuse to back down?*

*Those who answered yes to these questions are determined. These people have strong beliefs and fight to defend them regardless of the consequences. Often they are criticized by others, but those who share in their beliefs view them as role models. A person who fights for what he believes in almost always risks criticism from others. Does this sound like you?*

It might sound like you, but it also sounds like John Brown. Known as the man who staged an attack on the Federal arsenal in Harpers Ferry, Virginia, John Brown was considered a crazy man by some and a hero by others. In the state of Virginia he was found guilty of treason, and he was hanged for his crime. However, some people in the North saw him as a determined man working to defend those who needed defending—slaves.

On December 7, 1859, John Brown led twenty-one men, whom he had been keeping in his home, on an attack of the Federal arsenal in Virginia. He hoped that his attack would begin a slave uprising. It did not, and it led to the killing or capture of his men. Many claim that the attack by John Brown led to the beginning of the Civil War, which had been looming for several years.

John Brown's determination could be seen for years before his attack on Virginia. His lifelong hatred of slavery began when he worked to help with the Underground Railroad. Then, in the Dred Scott Decision in 1857 the Supreme Court ruled that slaves were not citizens but property. This angered Brown even more, setting his determination on a violent path to help to free slaves. He rebelled against those who crossed the border from Missouri into Kansas to retrieve runaway slaves, and it led to his murdering of five pro-slavery settlers.

# Civil War Personality Quiz 13

The sound of gunfire could be heard for miles, echoing throughout the hills. Battles raged in cornfields and beside towns full of civilians.

The day that Brown was hanged for his attack on Harpers Ferry he said, "Now if it is deemed necessary that I should forfeit my life for this furtherance of the ends of justice...so let it be done."[5] He was determined until the end.

## Helpful and Sharing

Is something only good when it is shared with others? Do you enjoy volunteering and donating to others? Does it bother you if you have something while someone else is in need?

Helpful personalities enjoy sharing with others as well as helping them. Often a sharing person cannot truly enjoy something unless it is shared with another. The reward is the sharing itself and not the recognition given afterwards. The same goes for helping others who need help. This type of person believes that it is her duty to help others if she has the ability to do so.

A person who risks her own freedom to grant freedom to others is a helpful and sharing person, no doubt, and this person is Harriet Tubman. Having escaped slavery through the Underground Railroad to find freedom for herself in Philadelphia, Tubman risked it many times by traveling into the South to help slaves gain their freedom. She brought her brothers and her parents to freedom through the safe houses of the Underground Railroad.

Harriet Tubman is recorded to have freed approximately three hundred slaves during the nineteen trips that she made to Maryland between 1850 and 1860.[6] During these trips she enforced strict discipline on those she was saving, even threatening them with death if they tried to turn back. Her strict code of behavior allowed her trips to be safe and undetected. In the ten years that she worked for the Underground Railroad she never failed at bringing a slave to freedom; every one she helped reached the final destination.

The most well-known conductor of the Underground Railroad, Tubman brought hundreds of slaves to Canada where they could be free. So high was the South's desire to stop her, rewards as high as $40,000 were offered for her capture, staggering amounts for that day.[7] Tubman was never captured or stopped.

Known as the "Moses of her people" Harriet Tubman continued to give after the war ended and freedom was granted to the slaves. She established schools where freed slaves could gain an education, and she spoke out for women's rights.

**Loyal**

*Do you stand by your friends and defend them even when they're wrong? Do you put family and friends before yourself? Are you uncomfortable with change, preferring to leave things the way they are now?*

*These are the qualities of a loyal person. Loyal personalities often defend those they care about even when they know they are in* the wrong. They put family, friends, and anyone they care about before themselves. Easily able to forgive those they love for wrongdoings, a loyal personality makes a strong ally. Are you loyal?

From the very beginning of the war, families were torn between their loyalties to their states and to their country. States such as Kentucky and Tennessee found it most difficult to choose a side since they housed a seemingly equal amount of supporters for both sides. Yet, loyal personalities made tough decisions and often caused rifts within their families.

Such was the case in the Steedman family of South Carolina. Charles Steedman was a commander of the army before the war began, and when his state seceded from the Union he was faced with a difficult decision. The Steedman family remained loyal to their now Confederate state, but Charles Steedman had pledged his loyalty to his country when he took command of his unit. Despite James Steedman's strong words that called his brother a traitor who had allowed "Northern principles to contaminate his pure soul," Charles Steedman formally announced his loyalty to the Union.[8] "I am as I have always been, a Union man—I know no North or South...all that I know is my duty to flag & country," Charles Steedman wrote.[9]

Other families were faced with similar questions of loyalty. Confederate cavalry leader Jeb Stuart and his brother-in-law, John Rogers Cooke, were native Virginians who chose the Confederacy over the Union. However, Stuart's father-in-law, Philip St. George Cooke, remained in the Union army and at least twice fought his son-in-law on the same battlefield. Another Virginian family, the Terrills, saw a split in loyalties. William became a brigadier general for the Union army while brother James became a brigadier general in the Confederate army. After they died in battle, the family wrote upon both of their tombstones, "God alone knows which was right."[10]

### Solemn

*Are you the serious one of the group? Do you worry about the world around you? When faced with a difficult decision, do you follow your heart but feel badly for the opposition?*

*If you find yourself lost in thought and preoccupied with the task at hand, you have a solemn personality. While solemn people aren't always serious, they know when to stay focused. They think things through and search for answers, often times realizing that there is no perfect solution. Solemn personalities take things to heart.*

Many words can be used to describe Abraham Lincoln, and *solemn* is a strong choice. To his friends, Lincoln was a joking and witty man, but to the public he was serious and close-mouthed. Preferring to keep to himself, Lincoln kept much of his personal life away from the public. Abraham Lincoln disliked his nickname "Abe" and preferred the more serious title of "Mr. Lincoln."

Abraham Lincoln had a warm personality, but he often appeared sad and melancholy. It is known that Lincoln dealt with bouts of depression throughout his life. He often said that his amusing stories helped him deal with his sorrow and overcome his sadness. Those close to him knew he carried a large weight upon his shoulders.

Lincoln was bothered by the great cost of the Civil War, both in money and lives. He was torn between his goals in life. On one side he wanted to reunite the severed nation that he loved, yet on the other side he devoutly believed that slavery must be outlawed. This stress could be seen on the president's face as he worked to bring an end to the war.

A devoted patriot, Lincoln put his job as president before any other. Lincoln's son had died twenty-one months before his speech at Gettysburg, and Mrs. Lincoln still openly grieved for her lost son. Before his trip to Gettysburg, she begged the president to stay home with the still grieving family. Despite her request and Lincoln's great sadness, he made the trip by rail to Gettysburg because he believed that his responsibility to the country came first.

During Lincoln's presidency he received criticism for more than his political choices. First Lady Mary Todd Lincoln was criticized for both her behavior as well as her family's loyalties to the Confederate army. Lincoln defended his wife consistently, but it was another stress on an already solemn man.

# Pieces of the Quilt

Through their needles women recorded history. By creating quilts that told stories of the war, donating quilts to soldiers, or using their needlework to raise money, the story of women in the Civil War can be told through a quilt. Read each piece of the quilt block and learn about women's contributions during the Civil War. Then, copy the shapes onto patterned paper and piece them together to create the popular pattern below known as North Star, named in honor of the star believed to have been followed by slaves seeking freedom in the North.

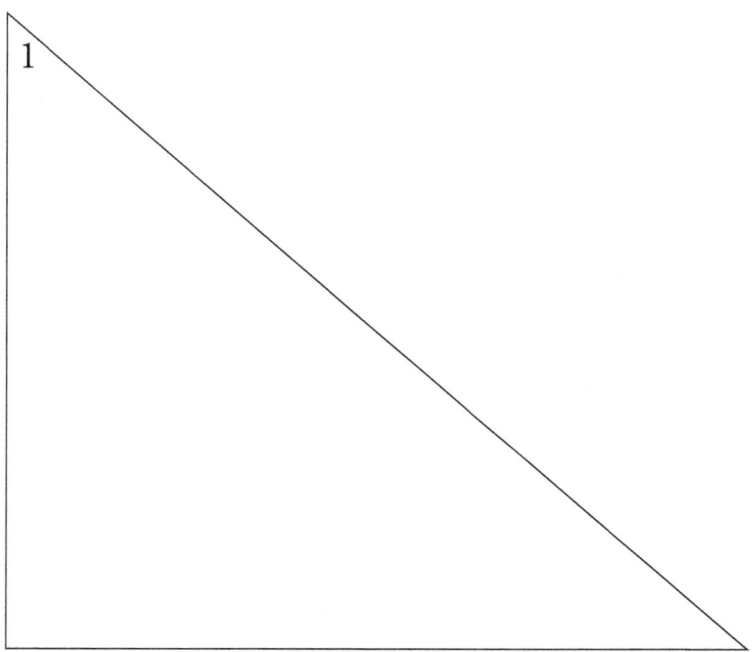

**1** Elizabeth Keckley used her sewing skills to earn herself freedom from slavery in 1855. She was born to a seamstress mother on a plantation and soon learned her valued skill well. A modiste, one who not only sews but designs clothes as well, she fell in favor with many while she worked. As times grew tough she supported her master and seventeen others on her plantation with her sewing. Many of the people who were so fond of Keckley were women of one of St. Louis' women's society who loaned her $1,200 to buy both her and her son's freedom.[1] Her sewing skills were then used to create quilts that were sold to repay those loans. Eventually, Elizabeth Keckley became the personal seamstress to Mary Todd Lincoln.

Other women sold their quilts for means of support, especially after the war ended and the South fell into poverty. Often the quilts were used in bartering for household supplies.

# Pieces of the Quilt

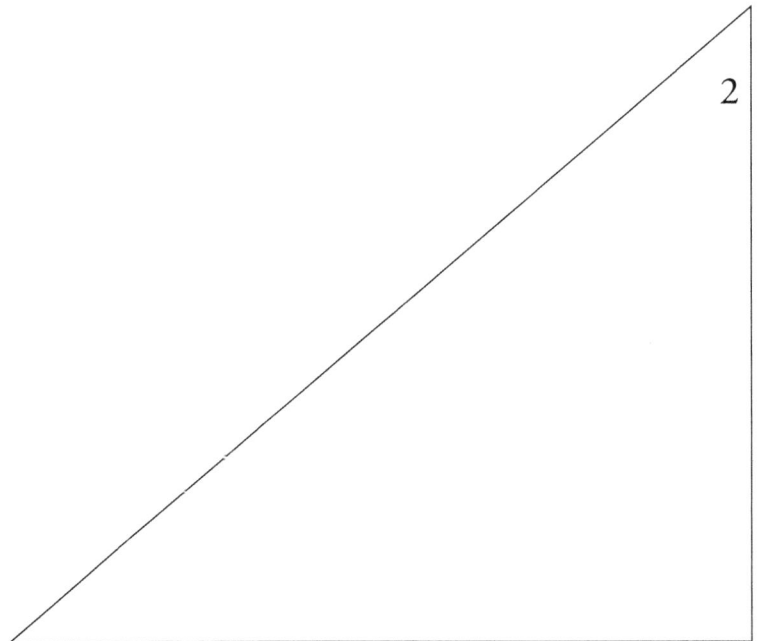

**2** Women could be seen on the battlefield for many reasons during the Civil War. During the time of the war many women served as volunteer nurses and an estimated 3,000 served as paid Union nurses. Immediate help for the soldiers was one of the reasons given for many men's survival after receiving injuries.

One of the less public jobs women had during the war was that of soldier. Under the disguise of a soldier's uniform several hundred women fought in combat. Because soldiers slept in their clothes and rarely bathed, discovery was easily avoidable. Most women were discovered after they were wounded and sent to the military hospitals set up in the camps. Some of these women joined for the same reason as the men—adventure and duty to one's country. Others joined to keep their families together while their husbands and sons were fighting. It is known that some women actually set up rough "households" in tents, serving in the same regiment as their husbands and sons.

**3** Women in the Northern states played an important role organizing the distribution of materials to the soldiers through the Sanitary Commission. The Sanitary Commission was a government association run by Union men. The women actually formed the Soldiers' Aid Relief, a women's auxiliary. This auxiliary began when the Northern women saw that the Sanitary Commission was receiving donations of clothing, socks, blankets, and other supplies for soldiers but was failing to properly distribute them, leaving them to sit unused while soldiers were in need of them. The Sanitary Commission claimed that its members had no time to distribute the materials due to their other war efforts.

Volunteering to take over the distribution of the donations, the Soldiers' Aid Relief began, and women took a part in the Civil War effort. They collected supplies to make quilts and other materials needed for the soldiers. Hosting small bazaars at first, they sold handiworks or personal items to raise money to purchase the materials needed to make quilts and other pieces for the soldiers.

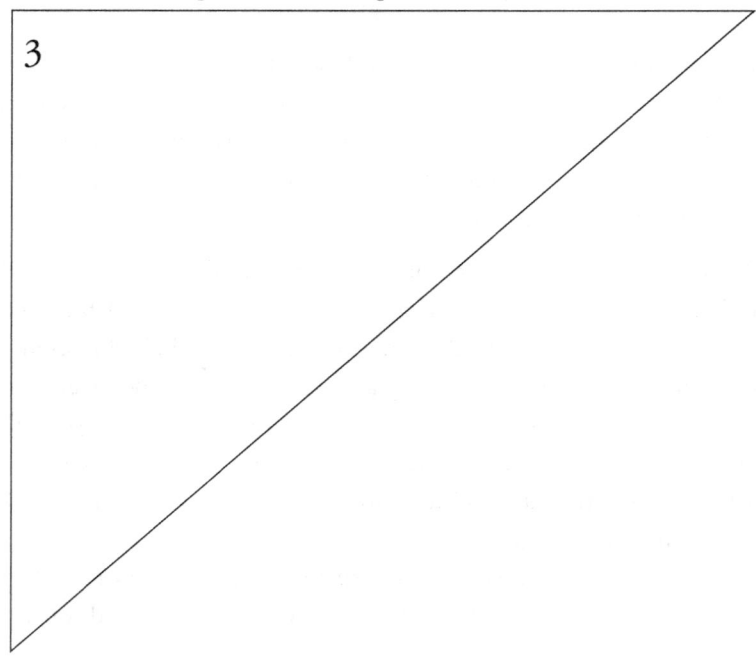

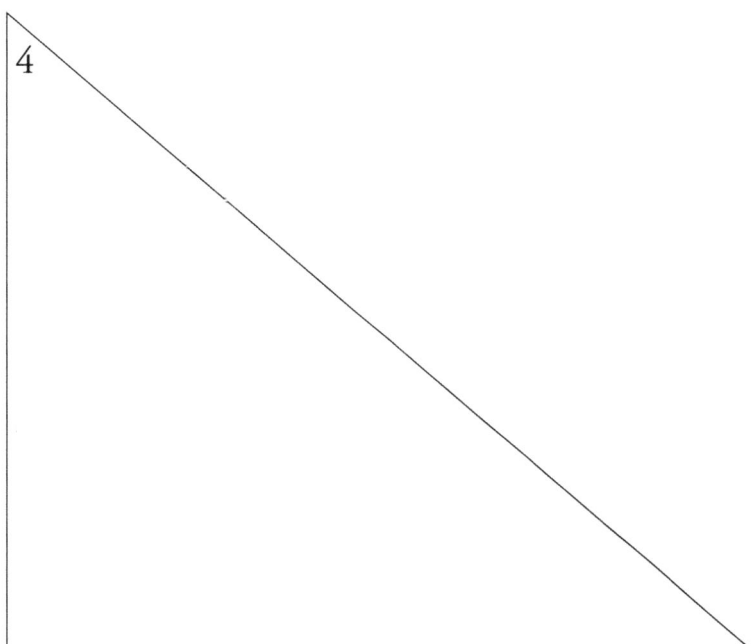

**4** Anti-slavery fairs were the Northern women's way to raise money for their cause, before and during the war. The first anti-slavery fair that was held in Boston in 1834 raised approximately $600. In 1845 the Boston fair raised $3,700, and in 1854 it raised nearly $5,000 for supplies.[2] In the beginning items were embroidered with anti-slavery sayings such as: "Trample not on the oppressed"[3] and "While our fingers guide the needle our thoughts are intense (in tents.)"[4]

The fairs also sold homemade foods and products, but quilts were the predominant items for sale. These fairs grew in number and size as the tensions rose between the states, making the years of 1861–1865 the most popular years for fairs. The first fair in connection with the Sanitary Commission was held in 1863 with the last being held in 1865. The Sanitary Commission estimates that the fairs raised approximately $4,500,000 during their operations.[5]

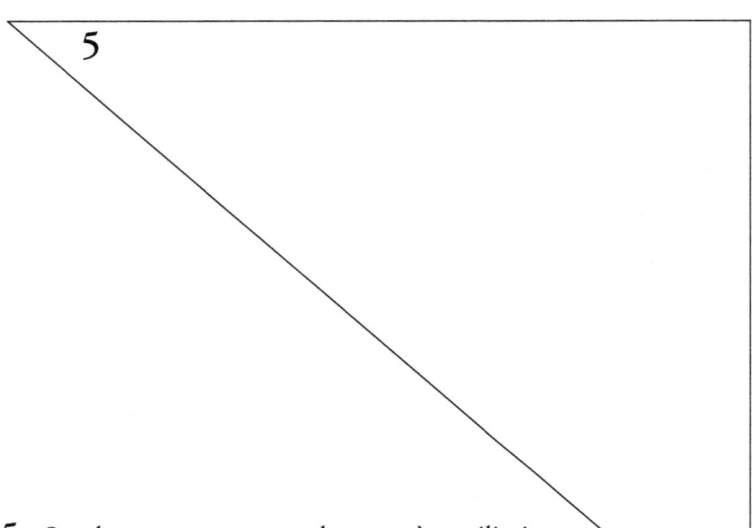

**5** Southern women created women's auxiliaries to raise money for the Confederate army as well. They held the same types of fairs to raise money, although none were as large as the Sanitary Commission's fairs in the North. Some of the quilts sold by these Southern women's auxiliaries were made in elaborately embroidered styles that showed the skill and time the women put into their quilts.

The first noted women's group in the South was in New Orleans in November 1861. Upset by the Northern capture of Port Royal, South Carolina, the women began their effort to raise money for a gunboat by selling homemade and personal items such as family jewelry. Groups even competed against one another to raise more money for their cause. The total amount raised was never known since little accounting was done.

With the North sending no textiles and importation cut off, the South was forced to find materials for clothing and bedding. Women's organizations that formed to provide boxes of clothing and bedding for the soldiers included the Ladies' Aid, Soldiers' Aid Society, and Ladies' Clothing Association. Later in the war fundraising efforts turned their focus toward medical supplies and hospitals for soldiers instead.

**6** Southern women sought to raise money for specific purchases rather than general supplies for the troops. During 1861–1862 Southern auxiliaries called Ladies' Defense Associations or the Women's Gunboat Funds surfaced. Intending on raising the $80,000 needed for a gunboat for the Confederate army, Southern women began a fundraising effort by creating and selling quilts.[6]

Although the money for a gunboat was never raised, enough money was collected for three boats: the *Charleston*, the *Fredericksburg*, and the *Georgia*, thus earning these boats the nicknames of "petticoat gunboats," which referred to the garments worn under women's dresses.[7] Although the excitement of this project was high at the beginning, it lost some of its power after a year or so when the North limited supplies to the South and naval success seemed impossible.

Fundraising efforts turned toward other needed supplies instead.

6

7 At this time soldiers needed quilts for bedding, and the faster bedding could be made the better. The fancy styles of quilts soon gave way to easier styles. Instead of pieced quilts made from several dozen pieces of fabric, quilts were made from whole pieces of cloth tied together at the sides, the quickest way to make a quilt. Southern women were limited since supplies from the North were stopped. Resourceful women looked to their homes for materials such as old mattresses, curtains, dresses, and even carpets. Color was important as well. At this time many rust- or brown-colored quilts were made with a darker print in mind for the soldiers. In the North especially, the patriotic colors were often seen in quilts, making them brighter than Southern quilts.

Northern women were asked by the Sanitary Commission to sew articles of clothing for the soldiers as well as quilts. The quilts made for soldiers were specified by the military to be approximately 54" x 84". Women did some calculating and learned that by cutting two existing bed quilts they could be sewn into three soldiers' quilts without waste. It is said that at the war's end nearly 250,000 quilts had been donated to the Union soldiers.[8]

**8** Many famous names are associated with the Civil War, and women are no exception. The war involved everyone, and that included men and women, wealthy and poor, famous and average.

One famous woman of the Civil War was Clara Barton. Known as the founder of the Red Cross, Barton began her work as an unpaid nurse during the early years of the war. After repeated requests, she was finally given permission to set up nursing stations at the sites of the battles. This early healthcare saved thousands of lives and changed the way injuries were tended.

Sojourner Truth was a freed slave who frequently spoke in public about freedom for slaves as well as equal rights for women. Her speeches were powerful, and she wrote the book *Narrative* about her experiences working for equality and freedom.

Not quite so famous, but earning her fame through her continued fighting was Jennie Hodgers, known to her fellow soldiers as Private Albert Cashier. Although Jennie was obviously female, she fought for the duration of the war as a man with no one the wiser. It is estimated that as many as eighty women were found killed or hurt during battle. If eighty were found, how many fought undetected? Hundreds? A thousand? No one will ever know.

> **9**
>
> The dimensions for this piece need to be doubled.

**9** Civil War history is filled with the men who were made famous due to their roles in the Civil War. However, women made many contributions to the war as well. Whether they were left home to tend to the household or in the battlefields tending to the men, women were noted as a crucial part of the war effort on either side of the Mason-Dixon line.

One quilt pattern is called "Sherman's March" after the famous campaign of William Tecumseh Sherman. It was created to honor what those in the South endured as Sherman's troops traveled over their homeland. During the march their homes were destroyed and their supplies were raided in an effort to force the Southern supporters to surrender. Most of these homes were inhabited by women and children who were left behind when the men went off to war. Today the injuries left behind by General Sherman's March are not as fresh, and the pattern has evolved to represent a newer idea. Today this pattern is often called "Churn Dash" to reflect the agricultural and domestic jobs of women in America.

Women's auxiliaries sold a variety of homemade goods to raise money for their causes. Canned foods and quilts were popular items.

Quilts were a popular form of recording history. Many reflect the concerns, beliefs, and materials available to the women of the Civil War. They also helped to pass the time as the women waited for the war to end.

# Fiction or Fact?

Myths about what did and did not occur during the Civil War are abundant. While some seem too unrealistic to be true, others are simply stories born from misinformation. Read each Civil War statement and decide if it is reality or fiction.

Fiction or fact: *Reporters from prominent newspapers disguised themselves as nurses or soldiers to get in the troop lines and collect eye-witness accounts of the war that were printed the next day.*

FACT It sounds like a scene from today, but reporters actually did sneak into the army troops to see firsthand what occurred during the Civil War. In fact, the Civil War is the first war in history to be covered by the press in the fashion of today. The telegraph had just been invented, and it allowed the reporters to send their information to their editors who ran the stories the next day. So many reporters filled the army lines that commanders worried about the security of army plans. General William Tecumseh Sherman actually threatened to shoot reporters who infiltrated his troops.

One reporter was welcomed; Mathew Brady had permission to follow the armies and document the war with his camera, providing photographic images of the Civil War.

# Fiction or Fact?

Generals on horseback led soldiers through battlefields. Today those generals and soldiers are remembered by statues that decorate battlefields across the country. General Winfield Scott Hancock overlooks Cemetery Hill in Gettysburg, Pennsylvania.

Fiction or fact: *Some battles of the Civil War have two names, a Northern name and Southern name. To this day those battles are referred to by either name.*

FACT The Union army named the battles after the closest landmark while the Confederate army named the battles after the nearest town that held their headquarters. This explains why the Union army fought a battle at Bull Run, named after the

## Fiction or Fact?

Bull Run River, while the Confederate army fought a battle at Manassas, Virginia. Both were the same battle. However, today the battles tend to be referred to by their Union names. This is because the majority of the newspapers of the Civil War were Northern, and therefore they used the Union names when referring to the battles. The names recorded in the papers are the ones more commonly known today.

Fiction or fact: *John Brown harbored twenty-one men on the Kennedy farm in Maryland in 1859 as he planned his attack on the Confederate armory in Harpers Ferry. While waiting, he gave his fifteen-year-old daughter, Annie, the job of watching out for visitors to his home. She often had to distract a nosy neighbor named Mrs. Huffmaster from noticing the "guests" in her home, and she spent most of her days sitting on the front porch steps serving as her father's lookout.*

Amidst the smoke and the smell of gunpowder, today's soldiers gather for a day of mock battle.

FACT Annie Brown was brought to the Kennedy farm in 1859 with her father. In order to hide the number of men in the house, Annie sat on the front porch during the three months they were there watching for visitors. One such visitor was Mrs. Huffmaster, a neighbor who posed a threat to John Brown's plan. Before the attack in October 1859, Annie and her sister Sarah were sent away to live with the Alcott family. John Brown was captured during the attack and later hanged, while most of the men who had stayed at the house, including two of Brown's sons, were killed during the attack. John Brown attacked in the name of freeing slaves, a battle he had been fighting throughout his life.

Fiction or fact: *While following the Underground Railroad, quilts were used to show the path of the railroad through their patterns. They also served to warn of danger or to indicate a safe hideout.*

FICTION The Underground Railroad refers to the organization of people who helped slaves escape to freedom in the North. This was dangerous both for the slaves and for those who helped. The members of the Underground Railroad as well as the paths taken while traveling North were a secret. While the use of quilts to identify these paths tends to be a controversial topic, there is no historical proof that quilts were used for anything more than blankets on the Underground Railroad.[1] Historians argue that it goes against good logic. If the patterns were known to show the path of the railroad, those who looked for the runaway slaves would have used the quilts to find the slaves. Similarly, the quilts wouldn't have been able to have been seen at night when travelers would most likely have looked for them. Instead, the railroad relied on conductors to lead the way to freedom.

Fiction or fact: *During the Civil War, not only was the country divided, but families were divided as well. More than a few*

# Fiction or Fact?

families had siblings who fought for the South as well as the North. Even Abraham Lincoln's family fought about which side they supported.

FACT It is impossible to count the number of families who were divided in their loyalties. One well-known family was that of Senator George B. Crittenden of Kentucky. He had two sons who both served as major generals of the army. However, one son was a major general for the Confederate army while the other was a major general for the Union army.

Even the Lincoln household was divided. Mary Todd Lincoln, the first lady, was from a family that supported the South. This meant that four of Abraham Lincoln's brothers-in-law served as Confederate soldiers. When the war was declared over, Mary Todd Lincoln was threatened to be charged with treason because of her family's loyalties. Abraham came to her defense and declared that she had no connections with the Confederate troops.

Fiction or fact: *General Thomas Jonathan Jackson, known as Stonewall Jackson for his determination, was shot by friendly fire. As a result his left arm was amputated. After its removal the general had a fully marked grave made for the arm, which was buried within the grave. When he died eight days later, Stonewall Jackson was buried in an entirely different grave.*

FACT General Stonewall Jackson did have two graves—one for himself in Lexington, Virginia, and one for his amputated arm in a family burial plot near Fredericksburg, Virginia. After a mistaken order to fire by a member of his army, Stonewall Jackson was accidentally shot three times by friendly fire from the 18th North Carolina Infantry Regiment. The injury caused his left arm to be amputated and buried on May 2, 1863. Jackson died from pneumonia on May 10, 1863, and was buried separately from his arm.

Fiction or fact: *Abraham Lincoln wrote the Gettysburg Address on an envelope during the train ride to Gettysburg.*

FICTION Although Lincoln only had two weeks' notice of the event in which he gave his speech, it is documented that he wrote the first draft in Washington two days prior to the speech in Gettysburg. He even wrote the draft on White House stationery. The final nine and one-half lines of the speech were added in pencil while Lincoln stayed in Gettysburg. On the morning of the famed address on November 19, 1863, Abraham Lincoln rewrote the speech, making very few changes from the draft that he brought with him.

*How did you do? Do you know your fiction from your fact? There are many other interesting stories of the Civil War that seem too unrealistic to be true. Can you name any more?*

A statue of Abraham Lincoln stands in Gettysburg, Pennsylvania, just outside of the hotel where he stayed the night he put the finishing touches on the Gettysburg Address.

# Letters to Home:
# The Words of a Civil War Soldier

Much of the information known today about life as a Civil War soldier was learned through letters. Soldiers wrote letters home or kept diaries to help pass the time, especially during the winter months when they set up more permanent camps. In the North the postal system prospered and even offered free home delivery for larger cities. By 1863 a standard rate of three cents was established. In the South, however, the postal system fought bankruptcy until its close in 1865.[1]

Letters were a soldier's only communication with home, and often they told of the real conditions in the camps. Imagine you were a soldier; what would you write in your letters home? Read these fictitious letters from a homesick soldier, Patrick, to his beloved sister at home to learn more about what it was like to be a Civil War soldier.

May 7, 1862

Dearest Sister,

Life as a soldier is not what I expected. The adventure that I longed for hasn't appeared yet, and so far I've spent most of my time as a soldier drilling. We drill at first rising, then we prepare our meals, do our daily camp chores, drill, sup, drill, drill again, and then lay down for rest only to dream of drilling. This is not the adventure I dreamed of while at home.

Tent camps were the homes of the soldiers for the months that they served in the armies. Soldiers looked for ways to pass the time in their camps, often drilling for most of the day.

I am glad to hear that you and the family are being in the enjoyment of good health. The camp here is a good one, and it is not so full of the sickness you hear. The men are good, and many are young fellows like myself.

We are here in wall tents that fit nearly twenty of us men. They say when we begin to march further we will only be afforded dog tents. I shall make my tent with a friend of mine who shares the same manner as myself. There is no room in the tent for more than the two of us. At times I long for the privacy of a smaller tent. The larger ones tend to capture all the smells that follow men who have marched in the hot sun all day.

I bid you well, fair sister. You are greatly missed in my heart.

Your devoted brother,
Patrick

November 18, 1862

Dearest Sister,

The weather here grows cold, and even our tents do not keep the damp from creeping in and sleeping beside us. We have been marching for days now, and it has at least delivered us from the daily drilling. I am far from home and the lack of Mama's cooking and the smell of the pastures is pressing upon my heart.

We were given our three day rations yesterday. Mine was the smallest portion of salt pork and toothduller bread. How I miss the fresh bread of home—the kind that is not tough and dry like this army bread! I am enjoying the salt pork today; last week we were given fresh meat which was still new with the taste of blood. At times it is pickled. There were no vegetables today, but I don't miss them. They are pressed dry and into patties so that they last, and I must eat them and not remember the taste of those from home.

I must now stir our fire and draw from it some heat.

Your loving brother,<br>Patrick

A contemporary captain's tent shows visitors how the soldiers lived during their service in the armies. With his modest bed and his uniform folded, it echoes the discipline of the soldiers.

February 9, 1863

Loving Sister,

    I am glad to hear of your betrothal to Jacob. I hope to say he fares better at this war than I am faring. At times the homesickness that I feel presses me so that I cannot walk another step. I ache to know that I will not see you at your wedding, but then I am grateful that the news is good, for I could not bear to be away from you and Mama if things were not well. Have you heard from Father? Where are his troops?

    Sister, I cannot tell you of the impression of war. How foolish I was to run off and become a soldier when I had at least another year of home ahead of me. Now I only pray that these battlefields do not creep towards you. To see what was left of it

The fife player announces the commencement of the battle.

stirred a hurt in me knowing that it had been someone's home not a few days before. Everything—the barns, house, and paddocks—were in ruins. The animals were butchered by cannon fire, and the land was ruined by the fallen men. It is not what I wish to write in this letter.

I shall go now. The musicians are rendering a version of "All Quiet Along the Potomac," and I shall enjoy its sounds for the moment. There is little to do to pass the time but write to you and listen to the musicians. My tent mate spends his time writing in his diary. I'm sure it is filled with the same things that fill these letters.

Fondly,<br>Patrick

June 1, 1863

Honorable Sister,

How I have now taken to counting the days until I can return home. We have been fighting in several battles now, and I am lucky enough to return at the end of each. Yet, the biggest battle I fight now is missing you and all that I knew as home. Pray, tell me that nothing has changed.

They say that homesickness can kill a man, and I believe it. I share a tent no longer. My friend succumbed to a sickness that he contracted from a broken heart. Homesickness filled his stomach and he no longer ate, making him weak and attractive to the diseases that run through this camp. We all began as healthy men, but now we look more like stray dogs all filled with fleas. They say we must bathe weekly, but I know men who have not touched water except for the times we march through streams. They are crawling with the graybacks that live in their hair, and there is little we can do to keep them from us. Some troops are falling not from rifles and bayonettes but from measles and chicken pox. I haven't seen either of them here, but it is only a matter of time.

I shall rest now, Sister. We reach Gettysburg tomorrow.

Ever-loving,<br>Patrick

July 5, 1863

Caring Sister,

My letter is to be short as I do not have the time I once had to write. Our battle at Gettysburg was long and few men I know escaped unharmed. Many lie in their graves in those fields, and I hear rumor that this was the deadliest battle ever fought on American soil. I have but one regret—to tell you that I am one of the men who have fallen to injury, and I am here in these medical tents. The nurses are caring for me, but it is not an easy road to recovery for me. Infection is what I fear the most. I will try my hardest to heal, dear sister, for they say when I am strong enough I shall return home to your care. How I long for that day!

Until then,<br>Patrick

Because supplies were limited, Confederate soldiers often wore civilian clothes rather than the typical Confederate gray uniforms.

# Which Is Which?
## North versus South

Imagine that you have just acquired a job as a curator in a Civil War museum. Your job is to organize and set up the exhibits that will be on display to the public. On your first day the owner, your boss, tells you that he would like to add a wing to the museum and it is your job to find new items for the wing. As a lover of Civil War artifacts, you know exactly where to look to find new items, but the hard part is labeling them as either Union or Confederate. Can you distinguish if these objects are Union or Confederate artifacts?

**The Weapon of Choice**

*A collector of antique guns has had a Whitworth rifle in his collection for years and he has offered to sell it to your museum. You are anxious to purchase the piece, and you are sure that it is a Civil War rifle, but how do you know whether it was used by a Northern or Southern soldier?*

It is a tough decision since rifles were often "captured" during battle. In the beginning of the war, both the Union and the Confederate armies imported a large number of rifles for use in their armies. These included a variety with bayonets mostly from England. Yet, as the war continued, various rifles were used. Short-barreled guns were popular with cavalrymen. Soldiers in general

A variety of rifles were used during the war. Often the Confederate soldiers carried imported rifles while the Union states made their own rifles.

soon learned that the bayonets served as better meat skewers than weapons.

The Confederate army, however, continued to carry European rifles due to their lack of machinery and materials needed to make their own rifles. The majority of their weapons were foreign imports or captured Union weapons. The Whitworth rifle was manufactured in England, and it was considered to be a Southern rifle. You are safe in placing this one in your Confederate display.

### Buttons or Belts?

*There is a farmer in Virginia who has volunteered to donate anything of value found in his barn. While searching through the*

# Which Is Which? North vs. South　　　　　　　　　　47

boxes stored there, you find a large brass button. It is round with a design pressed into the front. The design shows a scroll in front of a spreading tree with full roots. You think this might be a button designed to tell the soldier's allegiance, but you've never seen anything like it before. Is it a Union button or a Confederate button?

Both the Union and Confederate armies wore buttons to identify not only on what side of the war they were fighting but also their regiment. Union buttons most often portrayed the Federalist eagle in various designs. Confederate buttons varied in the designs as well. At the end of the war these were the only souvenirs that many soldiers could save from their tattered uniforms.

However, what you've found isn't a button but rather a belt plate. Used to fasten the equipment belts together, these are better known today as belt buckles. The buckle that you found belonged to a soldier in an Alabama regiment.

## Scouring the Fields

*Together you and your grandfather share a love of the Civil War. You remember vacationing with Grandpa in Gettysburg, Pennsylvania, when you were younger and searching the fields for buried Civil War bullets. You decide to ask Grandpa for a donation, and he proudly gives you a bullet that he found in the fields when he was a young boy. The bullet is pointed at the tip and flattened at the bottom with two grooves at the base of it. The grooves make it look as if it has an inserted base, but it does not. Did Grandpa find a Southern or a Northern bullet?*

A common sight after a battle, a bullet lies among the blades of grass on an abandoned battlefield.

Because of the variety of weapons used during the Civil

War this question is difficult to answer. Each weapon used required a specific bullet. However, Grandpa did well when he found this bullet. Known as a Gardner bullet, this bullet is definitively Southern. The Gardner bullet is the only one with two grooves at the bottom. Even more defining is the fact that this type of bullet was only ever made in the South, and it was only made during the years of the Civil War.

**The Shirt off His Back**

*Buried beneath piles of antique dresses, one collector finds a Civil War uniform. She eagerly donates it to your museum, but she knows nothing about it. The uniform is unlike any regulation Union or Confederate uniform you've seen. The pants are baggy and shorter than most. The coat is short too with yellow trim, and the hat is a fez rather than a cap. Your guess is that it is Confederate since the Southern soldiers were known to stray away from the regulation uniform more than the Northern soldiers. But how can you be sure?*

The uniform that was donated is not Confederate, although your guess was a good one. The Confederate army wore a variety of colors in their uniforms to the point where a complete uniform in gray was rare. Union soldiers tended to wear their regulation blue uniforms more frequently.

Special units were the ones that strayed from the standard uniform, and this uniform is from one of those units. Known as the Zouaves, the units dressed in French-Algerian style like the unit of the French army in Africa from where the Zouaves originated. Their coats were shorter and showed trim known as frogging. Their trademark pantaloons, often red, were full and baggy with white leggings underneath, and often the uniforms were completed with sashes. Hats varied from fezzes to turbans to tasseled caps.

Although there were Zouave units on both the Union and the Confederate sides of the war, the Confederate Zouave units gave up their excessive uniforms for the most part after the first year of the war. The Union Zouaves maintained their attire throughout the war, making the chances of this being a Union Zouave uniform strong.

Company Commander Stan McGee portrays a 146th New York Zouave during a reenactment drill. Zouave uniforms varied based upon their unit.

During a reenactment, members of the Pennsylvania 23rd/Birney's Zouaves, part of Vincent's Brigade, march while wearing the traditional Zouave uniform.

# Sherman's March through Georgia

**Atlanta**

General William Tecumseh Sherman of the Union army began his campaign in Chattanooga, Tennessee, with 100,000 soldiers. His objective was to move his troops into Atlanta, Georgia, and take over the city in the name of the Union army. In Atlanta Sherman's army was attacked by John Bell Hood of the Confederate army.

After Sherman proved his success over Hood and burned most of Atlanta, leaders such as President Lincoln and General Grant strongly suggested that he follow Hood's retreating army and cripple them. Instead, General Sherman decided to begin his famous march through Georgia.

Sherman's plan was to march his troops across Georgia, destroying its farmlands as well as its other resources along the way. In the end he succeeded in his goals by destroying everything in his path toward Savannah, Georgia.

Cannon were pulled into position during battle. Here, reenacting soldiers clear during the firing of their cannon.

# Sherman's March through Georgia

**Atlanta**

General Sherman begins his march from Atlanta on May 7, 1864.

General Sherman writes, "I can make the march, and make Georgia howl."[1]

**Milledgeville**

Sherman divides his troops into two columns of men headed in the same direction. One column was under the command of General Oliver O. Howard, and the other column was under the command of General Henry W. Slocum. During the march Sherman only supplied his men with bread, making them "live off the land" as they marched and harvested their food and supplies from farms along the way.[2] Bummers, as the men were called, set out each morning to steal whatever could be found as well as to burn buildings and to destroy the railroad. This would stop food from being brought into the towns. Sherman hoped that all of this would cause the Confederate soldiers to abandon their army and come home to protect their land.

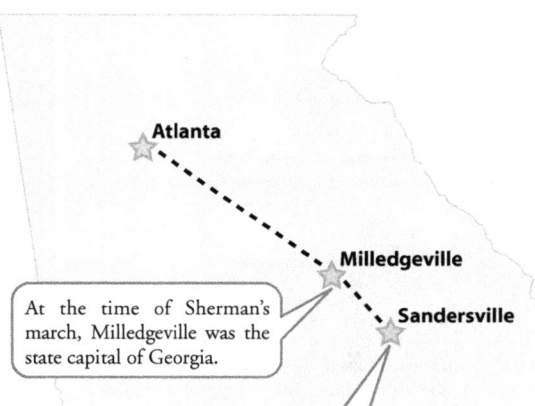

At the time of Sherman's march, Milledgeville was the state capital of Georgia.

While Sherman's men occupied Milledgeville, they held a fake trial, mocking the court of the state capital. In the trial they repealed the ruling that Georgia had seceded from the Union.

Not only did Sherman's men set fire to buildings in the cities they occupied, but they also ruined farms along the way and tore apart machinery. This ruined the commercial industry of the state as well as the agricultural industry.

A map and a harmonica helped pass the time during encampment.

# Sherman's March through Georgia

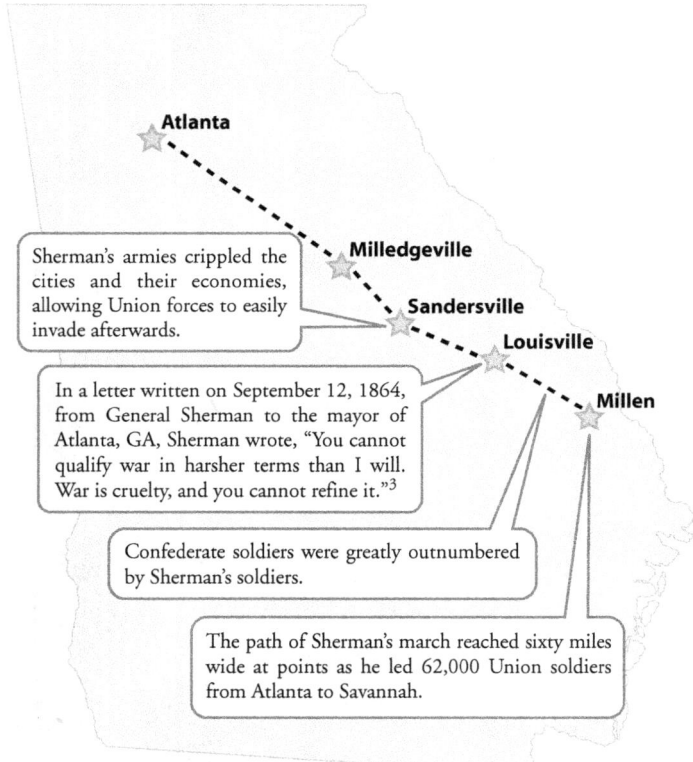

Sherman's armies crippled the cities and their economies, allowing Union forces to easily invade afterwards.

In a letter written on September 12, 1864, from General Sherman to the mayor of Atlanta, GA, Sherman wrote, "You cannot qualify war in harsher terms than I will. War is cruelty, and you cannot refine it."[3]

Confederate soldiers were greatly outnumbered by Sherman's soldiers.

The path of Sherman's march reached sixty miles wide at points as he led 62,000 Union soldiers from Atlanta to Savannah.

A Union soldier holds the tattered American flag after a Union victory during a battle reenactment.

# Sherman's March through Georgia

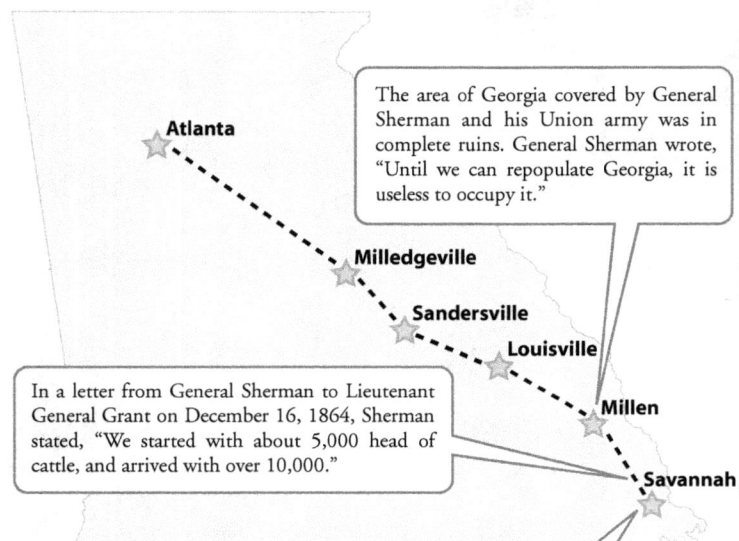

The area of Georgia covered by General Sherman and his Union army was in complete ruins. General Sherman wrote, "Until we can repopulate Georgia, it is useless to occupy it."

In a letter from General Sherman to Lieutenant General Grant on December 16, 1864, Sherman stated, "We started with about 5,000 head of cattle, and arrived with over 10,000."

Sherman's army finally seized the city of Savannah, Georgia, after ten days of fighting within the city's boundaries. During those ten days, the Union soldiers destroyed most of the city and ransacked the rice fields and the mills. The city was nearly demolished when the Union army evicted the Confederates and took control of the city on December 21, 1864. General Sherman "gave" the city to President Lincoln as a "Christmas present."

Sherman's Georgia campaign was over with an estimated $100 million in damages. From there he moved on to do the same in South Carolina, the state that most Northerners believed to have started the Southern Secession.

General Sherman wrote, "I do sincerely believe that the whole United States, North and South, would rejoice to have this army turned loose on South Carolina to devastate that state, in the manner we have done in Georgia..."

# Sherman's March through Georgia

General Sherman's March wasn't the only Union plan to "starve" the South. Cutting off Southern supplies was a successful Union strategy. At the beginning of the war General in Chief Winfield Scott expressed concerns to President Lincoln that the South could become prosperous as it sold its cotton crop to foreign countries. As the primary cotton supplier to the world, the Southern states could sell their cotton in return for military supplies. Scott devised a plan.

Known as the Anaconda Plan, Scott had a strategy to surround the Confederate states and block any foreign supply ships from entering them. Without enough factories to manufacture their own weapons, the South relied on imported supplies. Scott's snake kept the South without supplies while the North trained soldiers for the Union army.

*Map how the North limited the Southern supplies throughout the war.*

1. First Scott's plan blocked trade ships from entering Southern ports along the Atlantic and the Gulf coasts. Draw a snake that winds its way around the Confederate coast.

2. As the war progressed, the North continued to limit supplies from entering the South. Draw a wall at the Mason Dixon line, limiting supplies from traveling south.

3. Once transport of supplies to the Confederate states was limited, transport of supplies within the Confederacy needed to be limited. Draw lines connecting the capital cities in the Confederate states just as the railroads and supply routes would have connected them.

4. General Sherman and his troops have arrived in Georgia. Using your knowledge of his march, shade in the wide scar that his march made between Atlanta and Savannah.

5. By the time Sherman's March reached Georgia, part of his mission was to destroy the railroads that he crossed. His men pulled up railroad ties as they crossed the tracks, ruining the chances of rail travel. Some Southerners even called the bent rails that lay behind "Sherman's neckties." Draw blockades across the inter-city connections (the lines you drew in step 3) that intersect Sherman's March.

6. Knowing the limitations of Southern supplies, are there any other ways that the Southern states could get their supplies? Overall, explain the strategy of the Northern states.

# Civil War Trivia

Take this Civil War trivia quiz and see how well you know the lesser known facts of the war. As you answer each question, tally your score to see how you fare in the end.

100 pts. *What major health care practices were begun in the Civil War that we still use today?*

Answer: Health care changed drastically during the Civil War. While there are many answers, the more prominent one is

A surgeon's medical kit shows the simplicity of medicine at the time. Many soldiers were severely wounded during the war, causing them to lose limbs and return home with crutches and bandages.

the use of immediate medical care. Doctors realized that if a wound were cared for immediately there was less of a risk of infection or other complications. By setting up hospital tents near the site of the battlegrounds, the wounded soldiers could be cared for immediately. Before this the wounded were cared for after the battle was over, often times too late for the medical care to be of any help. It is said that by providing immediate health care thousands of lives were saved during the Civil War.

200 pts. *Which political party was formed during the Civil War?*

Answer: The Republican Party was formed in 1854, before the Civil War began. It was created on the basis that it was to fight slavery. Abraham Lincoln was the first Republican president of the United States.

300 pts. *What aerial device was used by the North to see over great distances but was never successfully used by the South?*

Answer: The hot air balloon was used to see over great distances by launching it into the air and then telegraphing the information to the ground. Dr. Thaddeus Sobieski Constantine Lowe launched the *Enterprise* on June 18, 1861. It traveled 500 feet into the air where it telegraphed a message to Abraham Lincoln.

The South never successfully used a hot air balloon to observe the Northern armies. One story is that Southern women donated their silk dresses to create a balloon that required the rare material for its skin. Since the Northern army had cut off trade to the South, silk was rare. Unfortunately, the balloon was captured during transport and it was never used. It was called "the last silk dress of the confederacy."[1]

The barrel of a cannon overlooks the serene fields of Gettysburg, Pennsylvania.

100 pts. *What do the Southern Rebellion, the War of Secession, and the Yankee Invasion all have in common?*

Answer: All are names for the Civil War. During and after its end, people were constantly creating new names for the war; there are more than twenty-nine names for the Civil War today. While the Southern names refer to what was felt as an unjust invasion of their lifestyle, the Northern names refer to their beliefs in the need for the war. In later years after the war ended, new names such as The War Between the States, The War of the Rebellion, and Mr. Lincoln's War were created that showed the war to be less devastating than it really was.

200 pts. *Where was the original capital of the Confederacy, and why was it moved to Richmond, Virginia?*

Answer: The original Confederate capital was Montgomery, Alabama. It was believed to have been moved to Richmond, Virginia, because Virginia offered the claim that it was one of the original thirteen colonies, giving credit to the lifestyle that the Confederacy fought to preserve. Many Unionists believed this to have been a foolish mistake because it placed the capital closer to the Union states.

**300 pts.** *What product had been manufactured by hand but was now being manufactured by machine, causing a protest by civilians?*

Answer: Shoes caused all of the problems. Having been previously made by hand, the creation of a new pair of shoes took time that shoeless soldiers did not have. Since machines could make shoes quickly, the demand for new shoes for soldiers made the need for machine-made shoes great. When the war ended, the machine-made shoes were here to stay despite the effort of the cobblers. Together they created the Knights of St. Crispin and petitioned Congress to stop the machine manufacture of shoes and save their jobs. Their petition was denied, and factory-made shoes are on the feet of Americans everywhere.

**100 pts.** *What great general was originally offered command of the opposing army in the war?*

Answer: Robert E. Lee was originally offered by Abraham Lincoln the position of commanding the Union army. Lee denied the position, following his heart and leading the Southern army.

Youths dreamed of the day when they were old enough to join the ranks of Civil War soldiers. Often the men lied about their age just for the chance to join the army.

# Civil War Trivia

*Your quiz is complete; tally your results. How did you do? Check the chart below to rank your knowledge of the lesser known facts of the Civil War.*

Less than 300 points: You may need to polish your Civil War knowledge base. Much of what we do today is influenced by the events of these four years of our history.

300–600 points: You're off to a solid start toward mastery of the Civil War. Keep reading and soon you'll learn why this war is studied worldwide by scholars.

700–1000 points: You know your facts! The war may have ended over a hundred years ago, but you know your stuff. You're on your way to achieving mastery of this part of American history.

1100 or more points: Did you serve under General Grant? Your knowledge of the time period is impressive, and you're a historian in the making.

# The Battle of Bull Run

The battle at Bull Run was one of the earlier battles of the Civil War, and both armies were inexperienced in the skill of war. Mostly farmers by trade, these men had little training but high spirits. Generals tried to keep those spirits high in various ways as the fighting of the war began. There were victories and defeats on either side, and although the Confederate and the Union soldiers had their differences, they also had many similarities. Read the following fictional descriptions of the Battle of Bull Run, also known as the Battle of Manassas, which could have been given by a Union and a Confederate soldier who were commonly referred to as Johnny Reb and Billy Yank.

**Johnny Reb**

The battle didn't look good at first. We were only 4,500 soldiers against nearly 10,000 Union troops. With our original ninety-day enlistments nearing an end, we were prepared to fight ruthlessly, knowing that it would be our only fight before we went home. No one wants to go home having lost; we wanted to return home as heroes. We had set up our camp near Manassas, Virginia, along the Bull Run River, and our leader was General Pierre G. T. Beauregard. General Beauregard was known for his lead in the attack on Fort Sumter, which is said to be the starting battle of this war. With uncertainty of what the battle would bring us, we set up our lines.

When the battle began it was more than we'd expected. The confusion of men and weapons left one feeling lost at times. The noise was overwhelming, and the fighting lasted throughout the day. As we tired, reinforcements arrived who could relieve us of our fighting and replace our wounded or dead soldiers. The reinforcements kept coming throughout the day, adding to our original number and making us equal to the Yankees who were tiring from the battle. For me, a farmer who signed on to fight for the Confederate army, the hardest part of the battle was identifying my own troops. Not only did each different band of soldiers have distinctly different uniforms, but also did the soldiers within those bands. Some wore the required gray uniforms, but others wore blue or even green. Amidst the smoke it was difficult to distinguish if the fire came from guns that were friends or foes. The battle flags looked the same too through the haze of the smoke. Both the Stars and Stripes and the Stars and Bars shone their colors and their fields of blue, but if the smoke covered part of one it looked like the other. I overheard General Beauregard say that when the battle ended he was going to set out to design a new battle flag, one with stars upon a blue cross in a red background.

By midday more bands of our reinforcements arrived, and the Yankees looked tired. When the band of soldiers arrived from Virginia with General Jackson we felt a surge of energy and victory amongst us. The general earned his nickname "Stonewall Jackson" during this battle because he stood firm like a stone wall. It was then that General Beauregard launched our counterattack on our worn enemies. We attacked with energy and the "rebel yell." The generals liked the yell because it mixed a native scream with a high pitched whoop. To yell it made me feel pride in the army for which I was fighting, and I would yell it as loudly as my lungs allowed. Our second attack set fear in the Yankees who retreated in a disorganized way, much

Confederate soldiers wore a variety of uniforms, mostly made of civilian clothes. The Confederate gray was not often seen on the soldiers once supplies became limited.

the way we were attacking. We had achieved victory this 21st day of July, 1861 both on the battlefield and in our spirits.

**Billy Yank**

We outnumbered them by over half. Not but a few hundred yards away they awaited our attack. We positioned ourselves at the Bull Run River, and this would forever be known as the Battle of Bull Run, at least that's what the papers already said. It was our first real battle, and we felt nervous and excited at the same time. General Irvin McDowell had brought us from Washington to attack the Yankee troops that we now looked upon. Our strategy was to capture the Confederate capital of Richmond, Virginia.

"Forward to Richmond," that's what we called our campaign.[1] Our spirits were high until we began our fighting. We believed this would be an easy victory, but then a few of us grew uncertain. Our short war seemed impossible, and our generals told us that we would win this battle easily and the Rebels would retreat. Our last war had been with the British and their fighting ways. Now we fought what had been our own countrymen not long ago. These had once been our brothers who fought with us for freedom, and now we fought again for freedom. Only this time we fought for the slaves' freedom from their masters rather than our own freedom from Britain.

At Bull Run we all fought hard, and we tired from our fighting that day. As the sun set in the midday clouds we lost our strength and our will to fight. Then, just as our last energies were being spent, the Rebels came at us like a swarm of bees, stinging our tired bodies. Many of us retreated in fear and panic at these immortal men, but then we soon realized that these men who attacked now were reinforcements who had been brought in throughout the day. We had only brought a scant few reinforcements and instead tired and injured men were being asked to fight fresh spirits. In the end we lost because of it.

# The Battle of Bull Run

Union soldiers wore more formal uniforms that reflected the colors of the Union army. Supplies were not as limited for these soldiers as they were for the Confederate soldiers.

In retreat we left that field at Bull Run and went home with doubts in our minds. Would the war really end in the ninety days we had been promised? Would we be as victorious as we believed? As I left that battlefield I once again heard the echoing sound of the rebel yell, and it did nothing but make me doubt my strength as a soldier once more.

In the end, it was the Confederate army who returned home in defeat. However, many Union soldiers did not revel in their victory. What had started as a three-month war turned into a four-year war, and soldiers on either side respected the fighting that the others had done. Together they would once again form as a union and eventually they would reunite as brothers again, but like the road home to the Confederacy, it would be a long one.

# Know the Famous Names of the Civil War

Many names were made famous by the Civil War: Ulysses S. Grant, Robert E. Lee, Harriet Tubman. But do you know the names of the people who were made famous by something other than the war? Match the famous names below to their involvement in the Civil War.

A. Louisa May Alcott, writer of *Little Women*

B. Walt Whitman, American poet

C. Dr. Elizabeth Blackwell, first female doctor in America

D. Jesse James, outlaw

E. Theodore Roosevelt, 26th president of the United States

F. Herman Melville, author of *Moby Dick*

G. Count von Zeppelin, inventor of the zeppelin and other dirigibles (blimps)

H. Woodrow Wilson, 28th president of the United States

I. Louis Pasteur, inventor of pasteurization

1. As a youth he rode with a group of Confederate supporters who left 150 abolitionist men dead in Lawrence, Kansas, in August 1863.

2. Known before the Civil War began, this man mourned after its end for the loss of President Abraham Lincoln in the poem "O Captain! My Captain!"

3. As an eight-year-old boy, he watched Jefferson Davis, president of the Confederate States, being taken by carriage to the Federal prison.

4. As a young boy he watched the funeral procession of Abraham Lincoln pass on Fourteenth Street in New York City on April 25, 1865. He watched with his brother who would become the father of Eleanor Roosevelt.

5. While visiting the United States in 1862, he watched a hot air balloon taking observations in Richmond, Virginia.

6. He seemed to refuse to take a stand on the war but planned to write a book entitled *Battle-Pieces* that followed the events of the Civil War through poetry. The piece was never written.

Aim was an essential skill. Battles put soldiers nearly face to face, and it was important to make every shot count.

# Know the Famous Names of the Civil War

7. While the Civil War raged in America, this man was busy in his home in France inventing a way to kill the germs present in liquids such as milk by heating them.

8. Her family took in Annie and Sarah Brown just before John Brown's attack on Harpers Ferry. She also served as a nurse during the Civil War.

9. She formed the National Sanitary Aid Association to recruit nurses to help the soldiers in the Union army.

The names and often faces of the Civil War are preserved in various monuments across America.

*Answers: 1.D 2.B 3.H 4.E 5.G 6.F 7.I 8.A 9.C*

# The War at Sea

The face of war ships was forever changed during the Civil War. The *H. L. Hunley* was a milestone as one of the first submarines. Yet, the greatest change was the introduction of the ironclad ships, the *Monitor* and the *Merrimac*. Before these ships all war ships had been made of wood. Now, iron was the new skin of navies around the world.

What drew attention to the ironclad ships was not only their thick, almost impenetrable, skin of iron, but the famous battle between the two original iron beasts. This was the first combat between two armored vessels. Even though Europe had ironclad ships to be built, none had ever been used in war until America used them during the Civil War. Although the *Monitor* and the *Merrimac* looked different, they were based on the same idea. Each was a ship covered with thick iron that brushed off enemy fire, and each ship reached a sweltering 140° inside. There is no clear-cut winner to the battle of the *Monitor* and the *Merrimac* because both sides believe that they won. The three-hour battle between the two ships ended when the *Merrimac* traveled up the river to avoid being run aground in the heavy mud. Meanwhile the *Monitor* changed command after the captain was injured, and it also changed its direction to do this. Both ships saw the other retreating and both celebrated victory. In the end, both ships were destroyed by the end of the war, but neither was destroyed by enemy fire.

Match the information to the proper ship's name. All three are ships of the Civil War, but each has its own distinction. The choices are: the *Monitor*, the *Merrimac*, and the *H. L. Hunley*.

1. This ship was blown up by her own crew when Union forces took over Norfolk, Virginia, where she was docked. The crew would rather have had it sink than have had the opposing forces take it over.

2. This was the first warship to have a spinning gun turret that could turn to fire at enemies rather than requiring the captain to turn the ship broadside in order to fire its guns.

3. Steering poorly mostly due to its enormous weight, this ship rode low in the water and looked like a "floating barn roof."[1] Its top speed was 4 knots, an equivalent to 5 mph.

4. This ship launched a torpedo that sank the *Housitania*. Unfortunately, the design of the torpedo hadn't been perfected and it led to the sinking of this ship as well. The torpedo was a charge of gunpowder attached to rope. When the rope was pulled tightly, the charge would fire. When this ship came close to the *Housitania*, it launched its torpedo into the hull of the wooden boat. Then, this

**The first iron-clad ships looked more like floating barn roofs than navy vessels.**

# The War at Sea

ship backed away slowly to set the charge. The problem lay in the length of rope, which was not long enough to let the ship get far enough away from the explosion. Both ships sank from the explosion.

5. This Union ship looked like a "floating shingle" with a box on top.[2] It rose two feet from the water, making it a difficult target, and it cruised at an impressive 6 knots (7 mph).

6. The original design of this ship was offered to Napoleon of France, but he declined the plans, leaving them for Abraham Lincoln to accept. This ship sank during a storm off the coast of Cape Hatteras, North Carolina, ten months after its first sailing.

7. A Confederate ship, it was officially called the *Virginia*, but most people referred to it by its original name. It first was a wooden steamer that had been converted into an ironclad ship over the course of ten months.

8. This 25-foot ship was made from a boiler tank. It held a torpedo at its bow and an eight-man crew. The ship traveled at 3 knots (4 mph).

9. This ship's first battle was with a wooden ship called the *Cumberland*. Upon ramming and eventually sinking the *Cumberland*, this ship lost its iron ram when it stuck into the *Cumberland*. It recovered, however, by sinking the *Congress*, another wooden ship, within the same day.

10. Two crews were lost in the first days of testing this ship. It wasn't until the third crew that success was achieved.

Answers: 1. *Merrimac* 2. *Monitor* 3. *Merrimac* 4. *Hunley* 5. *Monitor* 6. *Monitor* 7. *Merrimac* 8. *Hunley* 9. *Merrimac* 10. *Hunley*

# Twenty Questions about the Civil War

Have you ever played the game of Twenty Questions? To play you may ask twenty questions before you must guess the secret object. In this version the secret object relates to the Civil War. Ask the questions and read the answers to see how many questions you need to guess the secret object.

1. *Is it a person, thing, or event of the Civil War?*
   It is an event in the war.

2. *Is it a battle?*
   No, but it is part of what caused the battles to begin.

3. *Was it created during the Civil War?*
   No, it was created long before. It most likely began as early as 1619 when the first slaves were brought to America. It was, however, named in the 1800s.

4. *Is this thing large?*
   Yes, it spans a large area but it is not as large as many claim it to be. Its story has been greatly exaggerated as to its size, especially by slaveowners. By making it seem larger than it was, slave owners could argue for additional laws that punished runaway slaves.

Taking part in a reenactment on Little Round Top in Gettysburg, Pennsylvania, is Paul Miller of the Company "C" 2nd Regiment United States Sharpshooters (Berdan's).

# Twenty Questions about the Civil War

5. *Can it be heard?*
   Unlike the musicians that herald the arrival of the armies, this thing cannot be heard. It is almost silent.

6. *Can it be seen?*
   No, in fact it is said to be invisible. If it is seen it will no longer exist.

7. *Is it used mostly at night or during the day?*
   This is used mostly at night to take advantage of the secrecy that night offers.

8. *Is it used mostly in the summer or winter months?*
   Many say they use it during the summer months because travel is easier, but others say that they use it during the winter months because they are followed less. Since everything about this is secret, it makes it hard to know which months are more popular.

9. *Is this thing Northern or Southern?*
   It is a bit of both. While some Northerners are against it, many are involved with it. Likewise, many Southerners help it as well. It is located in both parts of the country.

10. *Does it have rooms like a house?*
    Yes, it has rooms but they're not like those in a house. It has secret rooms as well as trapdoors and tunnels that lead from one room to another. These rooms and secret passageways are found in buildings as well as wagons and barns.

11. *Is it a method of transportation like the wagon or the train?*
    Yes, it is similar to a train in that it has stations, railroad workers, and conductors. Some people involved are even called station masters. Yet, it is not a train.

12. *Does this thing take people places?*
    Yes, it takes people to several places that are all in the North. In fact, it once delivered people to places like

When soldiers went to battle, their wives and children often went with them, staying in the tent homesteads that followed the soldiers. Families had the choice to either stay behind and wait for the return of the men or go with them to battle, cooking their food and doing their laundry as the men went off to fight.

Philadelphia and Boston, but after the Dred Scott Decision in 1857, which allowed slave owners to come north to reclaim slaves, its destination changed. Instead of taking people to the Northern cities, it takes people to Canada.

13. *Do people have uniforms to wear while working with this thing?*
Sometimes the people wear disguises, but there is no uniform.

14. *How many people are involved with this thing?*
It's hard to tell. It's so secretive that no one really knows how many people are involved in it.

15. *Do we know the names of the people involved with this thing?*
Some. Names such as Harriet Tubman will forever be linked with this thing, but most will never be known.

Most people involved with this thing do so with much secrecy. Afterward, many of them change their names once they reach their destinations.

16. *Could people be punished for taking part in this thing?*
    Yes, people are punished severely for taking part in this. Those who run it could be jailed or heavily fined if the law learns of their names. For those who ride on this thing, punishment is much more severe. Beatings, maiming, or public humiliation are common punishments, as is death.

17. *Is this illegal?*
    At the time that it ran, yes. It was considered stealing, and those who helped with it were considered partners in the theft.

18. *Do people die while being involved with this?*
    Yes, many people do not make it to their destinations. It is dangerous to be involved with this, and those people who are against it are not the only dangers. Animals, weather, and other natural enemies make this a difficult trip.

19. *Does this thing use code language?*
    Yes, codes are used to indicate safe stops as well as upcoming danger. The codes are simple things such as hand gestures and noises.

20. *Is it the Underground Railroad?*
    Yes, the road to freedom taken by thousands of slaves is called the Underground Railroad. Hidden places along the route from Southern slavery to Canadian freedom are the stations, and those who help the slaves to escape are the railroad workers. Dangerous and always threatened by a party of slave owners who may be following, work on the Underground Railroad is difficult.

# Acknowledgments

I wish to thank the following people and organizations for their help in the completion of this book:

my husband, Robert, for his encouragement and help in finding the time to put this book together

my mother, Diana Diefenderfer, and my son, Christopher, for accompanying me on my many photo shoots

Chris Barebo of the 23rd Pennsylvania Volunteer Infantry, "PA-23rd / Birney's Zouaves," for all of his help teaching me about Civil War reenactments and pointing me towards great photos

Paul Miller of Company "C," 2nd Regiment, United States Sharpshooters (Berdan's), for allowing me to use his photograph

Stan McGee, Company Commander, 5th New York, Duryee Zouaves, for allowing me to use his photo

David Rider of Company "C," 2nd Regiment, United States Sharpshooters (Berdan's), for allowing me to take photographs of the troop

the 5th New York Infantry for allowing me to take photos

the 28th Virginia Infantry for allowing me to take photos

## Acknowledgments

the 21st Pennsylvania Cavalry, Companies A, B, M, for allowing me to take photos

the 23rd Pennsylvania Volunteer Infantry, "PA-23rd / Birney's Zouaves," a member of Vincent's Brigade, for allowing me to take photos

Pine Grove KOA at Twin Grove Park and campground, Pennsylvania, for its hosting of a Civil War battle reenactment and for allowing me to photograph the event

the town of Gettysburg, Pennsylvania, for its historical buildings, museums, and reenactments that were photographed and researched

# Notes

### Following the Code of the Civil War Soldier
1. Haskins, *The Day Fort Sumter Was Fired On*, 23.
2. Haskins, *The Day Fort Sumter Was Fired On*, 24.

### Civil War Personality Quiz
1. Davis, *The Civil War: Strange & Fascinating Facts*, 206.
2. Davis, *The Civil War: Strange & Fascinating Facts*, 207.
3. Davis, *The Civil War: Strange & Fascinating Facts*, 208.
4. Davis, *The Civil War: Strange & Fascinating Facts*, 208.
5. Cox, *Fiery Vision: The Life and Death of John Brown*, 201.
6. Ferrero, *Hearts and Hands: The Influence of Women & Quilts on American Society*, 70.
7. Levine, *...If You Traveled on the Underground Railroad*, 49.
8. McPherson, *Fields of Fury*, 22.
9. McPherson, *Fields of Fury*, 22.
10. McPherson, *Fields of Fury*, 22.

### Pieces of the Quilt
1. Ferrero, *Hearts and Hands: The Influence of Women & Quilts on American Society*, 45.
2. Ferrero, *Hearts and Hands: The Influence of Women & Quilts on American Society*, 72.
3. Ferrero, *Hearts and Hands: The Influence of Women & Quilts on American Society*, 72.
4. Ferrero, *Hearts and Hands: The Influence of Women & Quilts on American Society*, 75.
5. Ferrero, *Hearts and Hands: The Influence of Women & Quilts on American Society*, 79.
6. Cummings, "Gunboat Quilts: Fundraisers for the Confederacy," 3.

7. Cummings, "Gunboat Quilts: Fundraisers for the Confederacy," 3.
8. Ferrero, *Hearts and Hands: The Influence of Women & Quilts on American Society*, 77.

### Fiction or Fact?

1. Wright, "Hidden in Plain View: The Secret Story of Quilts & the Underground Railroad."

### Letters to Home: The Words of a Civil War Soldier

1. Jepsen, "Communications," 3.

### Sherman's March through Georgia

1. "Sherman's March to the Sea," 2.
2. "Sherman's March to the Sea," 2.
3. "Sherman's March through Georgia," 1.

### Civil War Trivia

1. Davis, *The Civil War: Strange & Fascinating Facts*, 55.

### The Battle of Bull Run

1. Haskins, *The Day Fort Sumter Was Fired On*, 31.

### The War at Sea

1. Stein, *The Story of the Monitor and the Merrimac*, 5.
2. Stein, *The Story of the Monitor and the Merrimac*, 19.

# Bibliography

Cox, Clinton. *Fiery Vision: The Life and Death of John Brown.* New York: Scholastic, 1997.

Cummings, Patricia L. "Gunboat Quilts: Fundraisers for the Confederacy." *The Citizen's Companion* (Jun./Jul. 2007) [The Quilter's Muse Virtual Museum] [cited 26 Mar. 2008] available from <http://www.quiltersmuse.com/gunboat_quilts.htm >

Davis, Burke. *The Civil War: Strange & Fascinating Facts.* New York: Fairfax, 1992.

Davis, William C. *Brothers in Arms.* New York: Smithmark, 1995.

Ferrero, Pat et al. *Hearts and Hands: The Influence of Women & Quilts on American Society.* San Francisco, Quilt Digest, 1987.

Freedman, Russell. *Lincoln: A Photobiography.* New York, Scholastic, 1988.

Graham, Martin F. *Blue and Gray.* Lincolnwood, Publication International, 2006.

Haskins, Jim. *The Day Fort Sumter Was Fired On.* New York: Scholastic, 1995.

Jepsen, Thomas C. "Communications." *Encyclopedia of the United States in the Nineteenth Century* 1 (Charles Scribner's Sons, 2001) In History Resource Center [database online] [cited 22 Dec. 2006]; Farmington Hills, MI: Gale Group. Document ID# BT2350040082.

Kiracofe, Roderick. *The American Quilt: A History of Cloth and Comfort 1750–1950.* New York: Clarkson Potter, 1993.

Kirby, Richard S. "William Cain." *Dictionary of American Biography, Supplements 1–2: To 1940.* (American Council of Learned Societies, 1944–1958.) In History Resource Center: World. [database online] [cited 20 Dec. 2006]; Farmington Hills, MI: Gale Group. Document ID# BT2310016600

Levine, Ellen. *...If You Traveled on the Underground Railroad.* New York: Scholastic, 1993.

McPherson, James M. *Fields of Fury: The American Civil War.* New York, Scholastic, 2007.

Murphy, Jim. *The Boys' War.* New York: Scholastic, 1991.

Rinaldi, Ann. *Mine Eyes Have Seen.* New York: Scholastic, 1998.

Robitscher, Jean and Naomi Dank. *Notable Men and Women of the Civil War.* Upper Darby: Precision, 1970.

"Sherman's March through Georgia." *Gale Encyclopedia of U.S. Economic History.* (Gale Group, 1999). In History Resource Center [database online] [cited 10 Jun. 2006], Farmington Hills, MI: Gale Group. Document ID #CD1667500635.

"Sherman's March to the Sea." DISCovering U.S. History. (Gale Research, 1997). In History Resource Center [database online] [cited 10 Jun. 2006], Farmington Hills, MI: Gale Group Document ID #BT2104241181.

Stein, R. Conrad. *The Story of the Monitor and the Merrimac.* Chicago: Children's, 1983.

Whitelaw, Nancy. *Clara Barton Civil War Nurse.* Springfield: Enslow, 1997.

Wright, Giles R. "Hidden in Plain View: The Secret Story of Quilts & the Underground Railroad. Critique by Giles R. Wright." 2005. *New Pathways Into Quilt History.* 11 Mar. 2006 <http://www.antiquequiltdating.com/ugrrwrightcritiqueHIPV.html>

Wulfert, Kimberly, PhD. Personal Interview. 25 Mar. 2006.

———. "The Underground Railroad and the Use of Quilts as

———. "Messengers for Fleeing Slaves." (2005) [New Pathways to Quilt History] [cited 11 Mar. 2006] available from <http://www.antiquequiltdating.com/ugrr.html>

———. "Quilts and the Underground Railroad Revisited: Interview with Historian Giles R. Wright." (2005) [New Pathways Into Quilt History] [cited 11 Mar. 2006] available from <http://www.antiquequiltdating.com/ugrrwrightinterview.html>

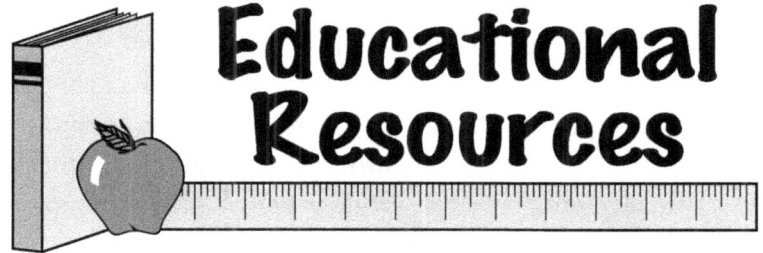

# Educational Resources

## Additional Activities

Follow-up activities make reading more meaningful and more fun. Whether you complete the activities for fun or you're a teacher who adapts them into lessons for the class, these suggested activities will help those involved to understand the Civil War even more.

### Following the Code of the Civil War Soldier

Southern soldiers were stranded far away from home. Imagine that you are a Confederate soldier in the North at the end of the war. Choose a hometown in the South and the location of your final encampment in the North. Using maps and today's roads, plot a path homewards. How many miles do you need to travel? Knowing that the average person walks 3 mph, how long would it take you to walk home? Factor in sleep and other necessary stops.

Another part of the Civil War soldier's life is battle. While people today may not be involved in hand-to-hand combat, we do fight battles each day. Whether it's a simple disagreement, competing for a spot on a team, or catching the bus in the morning, conflict is a part of our daily lives. Compare your daily battles to those of the Civil War soldiers and look for similarities between yourself and a Civil War soldier.

Create your own Civil War uniform. Try your hand at your sewing skills and create your own uniform after looking through some books with pictures of Northern and Southern uniforms. For a smaller project, create from paper or smaller scraps of fabric a uniform for a doll or action figure instead.

## Civil War Personality Quiz

Draw a silhouette of one of the famous people in this reading. After reading more about the person, fill the silhouette with facts about him/her. If a silhouette is too difficult to draw, choose a shape that best represents the person.

Many of the qualities that were admired in the people in this reading are present in people today. What famous people today share these qualities? Choose one modern figure of history and identify his/her best-known characteristic.

What characteristics are most desirable in people? The pillars of character are responsibility, caring, citizenship, fairness, respect, and trustworthiness. Are there other qualities that make people admirable?

Write a letter advising a Civil War figure of your choice to improve upon a certain character quality. Advise what plan of action should be taken and persuade the person to follow your advice to achieve this admirable quality. Consider the person's personality when you do this and try to explain things in a way that would best convince him/her.

## Pieces of the Quilt

Women earned money for their armies by canning homemade preserves. Try canning at home. There are many methods

# Educational Resources

and recipes to be found in cookbooks. You and an adult can create jars of jelly, fruit preserves, and vegetables.

Women made substantial contributions to the Civil War. Similarly, women worked during World War II to make such contributions. How did these Civil War women influence the future generations of women and those involved in future wars?

Quilting and geometry share concepts. Cut geometric shapes and use them to create a quilt square. Then, explain how you created the quilt square using geometric terms. You might discuss basic geometric shapes, measure the angles found in the quilt, or identify the types of symmetry found in the pattern.

When women were creating quilts to send with soldiers, they didn't have time to embroider or add embellishment to their quilts. Soldiers' quilts were often hand tied. Create your own hand tied quilt or pillow. Purchase two squares of fleece or two fleece blankets in different but complementary colors. Then, create fringe on both blankets by cutting four-inch slits around all four edges of each piece of fabric; the slits should be about one inch apart. Put the fabric back to back with a piece of quilt batting between them. Then, take one piece of fringe from one blanket and tie it together with the matching fringe on the other blanket until all the pieces are tied together creating one hand tied quilt.

## Fiction or Fact?

Brainstorm a list of possible names to use for the Civil War. Then, play charades with a partner to see how many of the names your partner can guess. (Charades is played by using hand motions instead of words. You may not draw or speak as your partner guesses what you are trying to say.)

The Civil War divided families as some people agreed with the Union and some with the Confederacy. What topics divide families today? Discuss these topics and their opposing viewpoints.

The Civil War was well documented with photography. Until then, paintings were used to capture the moments of the wars. While looking at some photos taken during the Civil War, examine these famous war paintings: *Washington Crossing the Delaware* by Emanuel Leutze, *The Sortie Made by the Garrison of Gibraltar* by John Trumbull, *The Battle at Bunker's Hill near Boston* by John Trumbull, or *Battle of Lexington, Mass. 1775* by William Barnes Wollen. What effect does photography have in comparison to paintings? Do they both try to capture the same type of moments? Do the photos create different feelings than the paintings?

## Letters to Home: The Words of a Civil War Soldier

Create a diorama of what Patrick's camp must have looked like based upon these fictional letters.

Many people leave home to go to college or to start new jobs. If you had to leave home and live somewhere far away, what would you miss the most? Why?

For one week write a daily letter to someone of your choice. In your letters include what has happened to you that day. Be sure to include worldly happenings that affected your day such as elections or news stories that impact you. Try to paint a picture of your life for this other person to read. Now put the letters in a safe place and don't read them until a month has passed. Did you capture your life in your letters? Put them away for a longer period of time and read the memories that you have saved.

Use the Internet to find addresses where you can write to soldiers today. Follow the format of a friendly letter and send a few letters from home to soldiers at camp or abroad.

## Which Is Which? North versus South

Visit a Civil War museum or another history museum featuring Civil War artifacts. Note the differences between the uniforms, weapons, and supplies of the Union and Confederate armies.

Today soldiers are issued standard uniforms and weapons. During the Civil War this wasn't always the case, especially when supplies got low. If you were a soldier, what five items would you be sure to have? Explain your reasoning.

The Battle of Gettysburg was the deadliest battle of the war. While exact numbers of soldiers don't exist, general figures work for this activity. Hone your mathematical skills. If there were 95,000 Northern soldiers, 70,000 Southern soldiers, and 2,400 civilians in town, what is the ratio of North to South to civilians? It is estimated that there were 51,000 casualties in the battle (a casualty meaning a soldier was wounded, killed, or missing). Of those casualties 3,000 soldiers are estimated to have been killed. What is the percentage? It is also said that 2 of every 3 Confederate soldiers were casualties; what are the odds of being a Confederate casualty?

## Sherman's March through Georgia

Imagine you are a newscaster who must cover the events of Sherman's march. Create a dialog for your broadcasts. What would be your headline for each day's events? Describe the footage you could use in your broadcast. Whom would you interview and what would you ask of them?

Sherman's march through Georgia was effective but devastating. Discuss the plan and its effect on the state as well as on the Confederacy as a whole.

How would daily life change for those who were left behind by Sherman's march? What daily activities are impossible after the march? What new chores would have been created by the devastation?

The idea behind General Sherman's plan was based upon economics. Without food and industry nothing would be left to support the towns and their people. Create a list of basic supplies that the South would need. Identify from where each of these supplies came. Are there any that came from the North? Which were available in the South? Behind each, mark if and how the North tried to cut off these supplies. How could the South continue to maintain its necessary supplies?

## Civil War Trivia

Learn basic first aid care from an organization such as the Red Cross, founded after Clara Barton visited Europe during the Civil War. What are the first steps of medical care after a person has been injured? What supplies should you keep around your house in case of an emergency?

Hosting the nation's capital city is an honor that each state would enjoy. Why then was the capital city of Washington established in the District of Columbia in 1791 rather than an existing state? How did this create fairness? What would be different if it were located in a Southern state? A Northern state?

Air travel has been on the move since Lowe's hot air balloon. The next evolutionary step of air travel was the invention of the zeppelin, inspired by Lowe's balloon. Look at the engineering feat of dirigibles like the zeppelin. What types of science are used to create these massive air ships?

## The Battle of Bull Run

Imagine you are going on a job interview after having served in the army. What qualities did you gain from your time in service as a soldier? How did this service prepare you for the world of business? Some desired qualities in the corporate world are: leadership, interpersonal skills, organization and planning, problem solving, using judgment, sensitivity towards others, and teamwork.

Soldiers of opposing camps were known to show friendship towards one another when not in battle. Northern soldiers even played cards with Southern soldiers while at camp. How do you think Billy and Johnny from this chapter would get along? Are there areas that they agree on and areas where they wouldn't see eye to eye? Can you understand the sympathy felt by the Union soldiers for their Southern brothers at the end of the war?

Billy Yank and Johnny Reb give two different views of the same battle. Imagine they were to debate the merits of their respective armies. Script a debate between the two soldiers about which side overall fought best in the war.

## Know the Famous Names of the Civil War

Create a concentration game that matches people of the Civil War to their accomplishments. List people's names on cards and their accomplishments on other cards. Then, lay the cards out on the table face down and play concentration to match them.

Read the works of Louisa May Alcott, Walt Whitman, or Herman Melville. Suggestions include: *Hospital Sketches* by Alcott, *Memoranda During the War* by Whitman, "O Captain! My Captain!" by Whitman, and "When Lilacs Last in the Dooryard Bloom'd" by Whitman. How do these pieces reflect the authors' involvement or thoughts about the Civil War?

Many future U.S. presidents witnessed events of the Civil War. How would this affect their future presidencies? What could be learned from the war, both negative and positive?

The Civil War inspired many inventions. Find some inventions that were created as a result of the war. What need was raised during the war that brought about the invention? Inventions can include improvements made to existing products.

## The War at Sea

Build a model of one of the Civil War ships. Remember that they were odd, looking more like roofs than boats.

Civilians stood on the banks and watched the battle of the *Monitor* and the *Merrimac*. What thoughts might have been in their heads while they watched? Did it seem real to them or like a play? Would some have been afraid to be so close to the battle? Discuss their thoughts and feelings.

Compare a Civil War ship to a modern-day battleship. Create a poster with a picture of the *Hunley*, the *Merrimac*, or the *Monitor* on one side and a modern battleship on the other. Label the features of each and note how many the two boats have in common.

## Twenty Questions about the Civil War

The Underground Railroad used codes to signal safety. Create some codes that could have been used to signal to the conductors that a stop was safe. Keep in mind that the codes can't stand out and must be subtle enough to go unnoticed by most except those who knew to look for them.

Those who ran the Underground Railroad did so to save people from harsh lives of slavery. Yet, their actions were illegal. What other people have committed illegal acts with good intentions? Discuss patriots of the American Revolution and modern-day martyrs.

Safe houses were built with secret rooms where the runaway slaves could hide. This is similar to those who hid Anne Frank's family during World War II. Research the Frank family and those who hid them.

## Overall Activities

Use a map of the United States and color the Southern states one color and the Northern states in another color. Don't

# Educational Resources

forget a third color for neutral states and territories. Order the Southern states according to their secession by writing numbers on each state. (South Carolina receives the number 1, etc.)

### Civil War Names

There are many names for the Civil War, some created during the war and some created after the war was over. Look at the accompanying list and decide which names were used and created in the South and which names originated in the North. Write the Southern names on grey pieces of paper and the Northern names on blue pieces of paper.

- The Civil War
- The War Between the States
- The War of Rebellion
- The War for Southern Independence
- The War of Northern Aggression
- The Third War for Independence
- The Second American Revolution
- The War of Defense of Virginia
- Mr. Lincoln's War
- The War of Secession
- The War of Insurrection
- The Slaveholders' War
- The Great Rebellion
- The War to Save the Union
- The War for Abolition
- The War of Southern Reaction
- The War to Prevent Southern Independence
- The Second War of American Secession
- The War
- The Late Unpleasantness
- The Lost Cause

Some of these names were more widely used than others. Which names were widely accepted? Why were some disliked?

Choose a few names for the war. Imagine it's 1864 and you're a reporter about the war. Choose a side, Confederate or Union, and decide which name you're going to use to refer to the war. Why did you choose this name? What does it say about your feelings towards the war?

Look at some archived newspaper accounts of the war, both before and after the war ended. Note the names they use for their reports. Which names are most widely used? Why? Do you notice a difference between the Southern reports and the Northern reports?

## The Battle over the Name—Northern versus Southern Names

The Union and Confederate states disagreed even on the names for the battles fought during the Civil War. The Confederate states referred to the name of the nearest town when naming a battle. The Union states referred to landmarks, especially bodies of water, when choosing a name.

### Battle Names

| *Known in the South As...* | *Referred to in the North By...* |
| --- | --- |
| First Manassas | First Bull Run |
| Oak Hills | Wilson's Creek |
| Leesburg | Ball's Bluff |
| Mill Springs | Logan's Cross Roads |
| Elkhorn Tavern | Pea Ridge |
| Shiloh | Pittsburg Landing |
| Seven Pines | Fair Oaks |
| Gaines's Mill | Chickahominy River |
| Second Manassas | Second Bull Run |
| Ox Hill | Chantilly |
| Boonsboro | South Mountain |

| | |
|---|---|
| Sharpsburg | Antietam |
| Perryville | Chaplin Hills |
| Murfreesboro | Stones River |
| Mansfield | Sabine Cross Roads |
| Winchester | Opequon |

## Famous Nicknames

Learn about the names listed below and match them to their nicknames. (Answers are below.) The nicknames were earned by their owners' actions.

1. General William Tecumseh Sherman
2. Harriet Tubman
3. Abraham Lincoln
4. General Thomas Jackson
5. Frederick Douglass

*Nicknames: The Great Emancipator, Stonewall, Lion of Anacostia, Moses of Her People, Atilla of the American Continent*

| Real Name | Nickname |
|---|---|
| Gen. William Tecumseh Sherman | Uncle Billy, Atilla of the American Continent |
| Gen. William Smith | Extra Billy |
| John Brown | Osawatomie Brown, Old Man Brown, Captain Brown, Old Brown of Kansas |
| Gen. George Thomas | Rock of Chickamauga |
| Harriet Tubman | Moses of Her People |
| Gen. Winfield Scott | Old Fuss and Feathers |
| Gen. George McClellan | Young Napoleon, Little Mac |
| Gen. Robert E. Lee | Marse Robert |
| Abraham Lincoln | Honest Abe, Rail Splitter, Great Emancipator, Long Abe, Giant Killer |

| | |
|---|---|
| Gen. William Jackson | Mudwall |
| Gen. Henry Halleck | Old Brains |
| Gen. Joseph Hooker | Fighting Joe |
| Frederick Douglass | Sage of Anacostia, Lion of Anacostia |
| Gen. Thomas Jackson | Stonewall |
| Gen. David Jones | Neighbor |
| Gen. Nathan Evans | Shanks |

Some nicknames are created out of admiration, and some are not. Look at well-known names of the Civil War and their nicknames and decide which were made by friends and which were made by foes. Look into key figures and explain how they got their nicknames.

Many famous names in history acquired nicknames. Look through the newspaper and find famous figures today who have nicknames that are used by the press. What inspired their nicknames? Are they friendly names or names intended to tease?

Do you have a nickname? From where did it come? What nickname would you prefer having? Are people in control of their nicknames, or is it something they earn without control?

# Index

## A
Alcott, Louisa May, 73, 75
Anaconda Plan, 59
anti-slavery fairs, 23–24
Atlanta, Georgia, 51–60

## B
Barton, Clara, 27
Battle of Bull Run, 32–33, 67–71
Battle of Gettysburg, 10, 42
Battle of Petersburg, 10
Battle of Wilderness, 10
Beauregard, Gen. Pierre G T., 67–68
Billy Yank, 70–71
Blackwell, Dr. Elizabeth, 72, 75
Boston, Massachusetts, 23, 84
Brady, Mathew, 31
Brown, Annie, 33–34, 75
Brown, John, 12–13, 33–34
Brown, Sarah, 75
bummers, 53

## C
Cain, William, 3
Canada, 85
*Charleston*, USS, 25
Chattanooga, Tennessee, 51
*Congress*, USS, 79
Cooke
 John Rogers, 15
 Phillip St. George, 15
Crittenden, Sen. George B., 35
*Cumberland*, USS, 79

## D
Davis, Jefferson, 74
Dred Scott Decision, 12, 84

## E
*Enterprise*, 62

## F
*Fredericksburg*, CSS, 25

## G
Gardner bullet, 48
*Georgia*, CSS, 25
Gettysburg, battle of. *See* Battle of Gettysburg
Gettysburg Address, 36
Grant, Gen. Ulysses S., 7, 51, 58

## H
Harpers Ferry, Virginia, 12–13, 33–34, 75
*H. L. Hunley*, CSS, 77–79
Hodgers, Jenny, 27
Hood, John Bell, 51
*Housitania*, USS, 78
Howard, Gen. Oliver O., 53

## I
injury/illness, 43, 44, 61–62

## J
Jackson, Gen. Thomas Jonathan "Stonewall," 35, 68
James, Jesse, 73, 74
Johnny Reb, 67–70

## K
Keckley, Elizabeth, 20
Kentucky, 15
Knights of St. Crispin, 64

## L

Ladies' Aid, 24
Ladies' Clothing Assoc., 24
Ladies' Defense Assoc., 25
Lee, Gen. Robert E., 9–11, 64
Lincoln, Abraham, 51, 64, 74, 79
  family divided, 35
  *Gettysburg Address*, 36–37
  personality, 16–17
Lincoln, Mary Todd, 16, 17, 35
Louisville, Georgia, 56–58
Lowe, Dr. Thaddeus Sobieski Constantine, 62

## M

Manassas, battle of. *See* Battle of Bull Run
McDowell, Gen. Irvin, 70
Melville, Herman, 73, 74
*Merrimac*, CSS, 77–79
Milledgeville, Georgia, 54–58
Millen, Georgia, 56–58
*Monitor*, USS, 77–79
Montgomery, Alabama, 63
musicians, 3

## N

Napoleon, 79
National Sanitary Aid Assoc. (Sanitary Commission), 22, 23, 26, 75
New Orleans, Louisiana, 24
New York City, New York, 74
Norfolk, Virginia, 78
nurses, 21, 44

## P

Pasteur, Louis, 73, 75
Philadelphia, Pennsylvania, 84
Port Royal, South Carolina, 24

## R

rations, 41
rebel yell, 68, 71
reporters, 31
Republicans, 62
Richmond, Virginia, 63, 70, 74
Roosevelt, Eleanor, 74
Roosevelt, Theodore, 73, 74

## S

Sandersville, Georgia, 54–58
Savannah, Georgia, 51, 56–58
Scott, Gen. in Chief Winfield, 59
Sherman, Gen. William Tecumseh, 7, 31, 51–59
Sherman's March, 9, 28, 51–59
shoes, 64
Slocum, Gen. Henry W., 53
soldiers, 1–8, 15, 21, 39–44
Soldiers' Aid Relief, 22
Soldiers' Aid Society, 24
Steedman
  Charles, 15
  James, 15
Stuart, James Ewell Brown "Jeb", 15

## T

Tennessee, 15
Terrill
  James, 15
  William, 15
Truth, Sojourner, 27
Tubman, Harriet, 14, 84

## U

Underground Railroad, 13–14, 34, 81–85

## V

*Virginia*, CSS, 79

## W

Washington, DC, 7
Whitman, Walt, 73, 74
Whitworth rifle, 45–46
Wilson, Woodrow, 73–74
Women's Gunboat Funds, 25

## Z

Zeppelin, Count von, 73, 74
Zouave, 48–50

# The Author

Kelly Ann Butterbaugh is an English teacher in both the public school and college setting. She has over ten years experience teaching in the public school system and over five years experience teaching writing at the collegiate level. She holds a Bachelor of Arts in English with a teaching certificate from Moravian College and a Master of Education in secondary English education from DeSales University. A freelance writer and on-line columnist, her writings have been published in *Learning through History*, *Pennsylvania Magazine*, *CollegeBound Teen*, and various other publications. She resides in Pennsylvania.

# — Award Winning Civil War Kids Titles —

### Slaves Who Dared
*The Stories of Ten African American Heroes*
Mary Garrison

**National Federation of Press Women Juvenile Book Award Winner**

Paints a picture of slave life and the courage the slaves showed in overcoming their hardships based on the narratives of ten influential African Americans. Included are Frederick Douglass, Josiah Henson, Harriet Jacobs, Sojourner Truth, Henry Bibb, Ellen and William Craft, and others.

ISBN 978-1-57249-272-1 • Hardcover $19.95

### Lottie's Courage
*A Contraband Slave's Story*
Phyllis Hall Haislip

**Beacon of Freedom Award Winner**

Many contraband slaves found freedom in Fortress Monroe on the Virginia Peninsula; hence the setting for this historical novel based on memoirs and other records describing the experiences of runaway slaves who found refuge at Fortress Monroe in Virginia during the Civil War. Life among the contraband slaves provides the basis for Lottie's struggle to overcome her fears and keep alive the hope that someday she will find her mother. Educational Resources included.

ISBN 978-1-57249-311-7 • Softcover $7.95

### Retreat from Gettysburg
Kathleen Ernst

**Arthur Tofte Juvenile Fiction Book Award Winner**

A Williamsport boy faces difficult choices when rising Potomac River floodwater traps the Confederate army trying to reach Virginia after its battle at Gettysburg. His patriotic feeling is tested when in caring for a wounded Confederate, he recognizes the humanity of the other side.

ISBN 978-1-57249-187-8 • Hardcover $17.95

**White Mane Publishing Co., Inc.**

To Request a Catalog Please Write to:
**WHITE MANE PUBLISHING COMPANY, INC.**
P.O. Box 708 • Shippensburg, PA 17257
e-mail: marketing@whitemane.com

www.ingramcontent.com/pod-product-compliance
Lightning Source LLC
Chambersburg PA
CBHW071300040426
42444CB00009B/1801